FRENCH HOUSE CHIC

FRENCH HOUSE CHIC

JANE WEBSTER

PHOTOGRAPHY BY
ROBYN LEA

Thames & Hudson

With each passing day I realise more and more that the little things
in life are actually the most momentous. Without the never-ending
support and love of my husband, Pete, for my hairbrained ideas I would
not be living and sharing this extraordinary life! x

CONTENTS

ROOMS FOR RETREAT

OFF TO THE MARKET

DREAM

FRENCH

DREAMING OF
A FRENCH HOUSE

t seems a lifetime ago and yet it has merely been twelve years. Twelve years since my husband Pete and I made that incredible decision to pack up our family home in suburban Melbourne and move lock, stock and barrel to an abandoned 19th-century château deep in rural Normandy. Looking back I sometimes wonder how we came to make that decision. There were so many reasons not to forge ahead with this wild dream, namely uprooting four young children, leaving our friends and family, fear of failure, fear of loneliness and finally fear of financial ruin! ⤙ Our family life changed overnight when we bought Château Bosgouet. Suddenly, as proprietors of an old house in France, we had to organise the relocation of our whole lives. We had four children, Lachie who was 12 at the time, Millie 11, Maddie 10 and Alex 4 – none of whom spoke a word of French. We had our house in Melbourne to sell and there was a lot of French bureaucracy to navigate. We were actually in negotiations for around two years before the notaires finally settled and we were on our way. ⤙ I will never forget that first day when we got the keys to the château and entered her doors as her new custodians. We pushed open the enormous heavy oak doors, all six of us straining to move them against the debris left by thieves who had recently broken into Bosgouet and left a trail of destruction throughout. My heart sank when I saw that all of the original marble fireplaces had been ripped out of the walls. Standing there in the entrée I remember assessing the enormity of this clean-up and thinking tremulously, 'What on earth have we done?'. But I knew I had to have an optimistic smile for the four little children searching my face for a reaction. 'This is not so bad,' I said. 'We will get this mess cleaned up in no time.' It was just the reassurance they needed to hear. They were off to explore and as the peels of laughter and squeals of delight began to ring through the house Pete and I began there and then to pick up rubble from around the front door so we could at least open it properly. It was not the last time I would have to put on a brave face to cover up my own nerves and terrors. ⤙ We knew we had about four weeks before every one of our worldly possessions arrived by ship from Australia. Before then we needed the house clean of all debris, old institutional furniture and dead mice! Our first days there in France were a whirl of gentle orientation to get the children into the local school, cleaning all day long and getting the hang of the pace and schedule of living in the French countryside. We had help from our caretakers, a couple around the same age as us who had two young children. They were on their own family adventure from New Zealand and they were a godsend for us. In another place and time we would not have found common ground but there in France we became firm friends and allies on a wild adventure together. ✐ I'm often asked what was the most challenging part of moving to France in the way we did. That's a hard one because there are so many aspects. Was it the clean-up of a huge old house that had not been occupied in ten years? I don't think so. It was hard work and seemed never ending at times but was it a challenge … not really. Actually I find that type of work incredibly satisfying. I remember tackling my favourite bedroom on the first floor. I had loved this room with its Versailles parquetry floors from the very first visit to Bosgouet. I could see the quiet charm of this room even beneath the years of neglect. Armed with industrial garbage bags, a brush and shovel, a vacuum cleaner, mop and bucket it was one of the very first rooms I tackled single-handedly. I crawled over every square inch of that floor using my little brush and shovel to scoop up all excess dust, dirt and grime. I then vacuumed every crevice and crack in the parquetry with the determination of a digger panning for gold. Not so different really as tucked tightly under a piece of parquetry that day I found a little cluster of rose gold St Christopher's medals all tied together with a bit of wire. I yanked them out from their hiding place and burst into tears, finally succumbing to the one real challenge I had been fighting for weeks, homesickness. ✐ Every time it appeared I would swallow hard, smile broadly and force it back down to a deep place where I hoped and prayed it would remain. But there I was on my bedroom floor and the monster had escaped and I knew instinctively that there was no way to capture this menace. I would have to fight him with everything I had. The children could not under any circumstances know I was homesick. I knew if they fed off my insecurities then we were doomed to failure. ✐ In fact, it was homesickness combined with a primal kind of fear. To fulfil what was essentially a whimsical dream of mine to live for a time in France, I had destabilised my entire family and our livelihood. Yes, we had some

Overleaf

A BEAUTIFUL LITTLE
16TH-CENTURY CHÂTEAU IN THE
TINY HAMLET OF JONQUAY.

savings but to properly restore the château and to make our home in France I would somehow need to generate an income. I had plenty to think about as I filled my days with cleaning, scraping, painting and polishing. Even small tasks such as shopping for food for the family were all-consuming because my French was still elementary. I only ever ventured out with a vocab and phrase list in hand. Even though I had moments of panic, I never let the children see this. I threw myself into every aspect of the project portraying a positive, relentless work ethic, only falling apart occasionally while the children were at school and I was alone with Pete. And while I now have the benefit of hindsight and can unequivocally say that our life in France enriched us in every single way, it was much harder to see the forest for the trees in those early days. Almost every day in those first two years I questioned why I had done this to my family. But somewhere, deep beneath my worries and the day-to-day busyness and physical labour of bringing a house back to life, I had a committed belief that if you are chasing a dream that is almost an integral part of who you are then it must, at some point, all fall into place.

The children had their own challenges, which were somewhat watered down as we had said, 'Just make friends and learn the language. Don't worry about anything else. If you are behind in maths when we get back to Australia, Dad can catch you up.' Those two years in France were filled with games and fun unlike anything they had ever dreamed of. They explored the rambling old house and the forest, rolled on the endless grass of the château lawns, made huge bonfires with their father, made movies, laughed, cried and made friends with village children. I'm not going to pretend that they loved school, but all four of them went happily enough each morning and I was waiting at the gate for them every evening to listen to the woes and occasional achievements that met our four little Australians on a daily basis. France gave our children a resilience, an independence and a determination that has dominated each and every one of them throughout their teen years and into adulthood.

Our containers of furniture and household goods arrived from Australia. Much of it looked immediately at home, strangely enough. The cream sofas that I had bought at Leonard Joel's auction house and that had sat so neatly in my house in Melbourne filled the gracious spaces of my French sitting room easily. The collections of crockery and cutlery that I had carefully built up over the years were happily put to use in France and the tables and armoires looked as though they were made for Bosgouet. As I unpacked the crates and boxes and found myself once again surrounded by so many treasured possessions, all looking surprisingly at home in this grander version of anything I had ever lived in, an idea began to emerge.

The year was 1990. As we sped through the French countryside, with my nose pressed firmly on the window of the TGV, I saw one for the first time. Pete and I were on our honeymoon in Paris and had decided we would leave the heat of the city and venture further afield to Beaune. The hot, late summer sun was shining brightly in the clearest blue sky when I noticed dappled sunlight shining through a thick forest. Not a random forest but somehow ordered and patterned, and it caught my eye immediately. I elbowed my new husband without taking my eye off the groupings of tall oaks for a second, and just as I nudged Pete he turned in the same direction and we saw it together. Peeking through the rows of carefully planted French oaks we glimpsed – fleetingly – our first French château. The house stood as solid as a rock, commanding the park with a mansard slate grey roof and Napoleon III symmetry. Dilapidated peeling shutters were locked tight and there seemed to be no sign of human life – just order and age and presence. I found myself wondering what lay behind those shutters. Who lived there and looked after a house like that? ⋙ It was the highlight of our three weeks in France and something I will never forget. It was on that train, on that very day, that it all began. It was like my five senses were truly alive for the first time. There was a change in me that day, a shift in the way I looked at life and the world at large. My French dream began that September so many years ago and set me on an adventure unlike anything

I could have imagined for myself. ❧ Some might say it was the beginning of an obsession but I prefer to think of it as a crossroads that I had been heading towards all my life. I wondered why I was so attracted to these grand old French châteaux and why I felt as though I had found my spiritual home when I was in France. I suppose it's obvious now that with antique dealers as parents, I would have an appreciation of furniture and objects and the patina of age. ❧ Growing up with parents as antique dealers was a bittersweet experience. Long drives in the back of the station wagon to that elusive next auction, and scrounging in and through huge piles of furniture at auctions, trash-and-treasure markets and antique stores in lonely country lanes throughout Australia. Mostly fun but when you are a little kid it seems like a strange thing to do to fill your hours. Of course nowadays I see it as a gift. I certainly would not be the person I am or doing the exciting work I do if it had not been for those eclectic, early years learning the auction game at the knees of my parents. ❧ I was quite young when my parents, Doug and Aileen, began renovating our family home – perhaps 6 or 7. The architect working with them was enamoured with my mother's talent for design. She had a style all of her own and our suburban Melbourne house was an eclectic mix of modern, antique and whimsical. There were beautiful chandeliers in all the main rooms as well as smaller versions in our bedrooms, antique furniture from many different eras and countries, and beautiful china that was displayed and never used. Mum bought paintings from country stores when we went on our Sunday drives into rural Victoria. She found copper pots, tapestries, Victorian washboards that my father would carefully wax and polish, antique china dolls and silver candelabras. ❧ My mother had such a way of putting things together that the architect working on our renovation asked her to become a partner in his business. In retrospect I think this was her crossroad. I remember serious, muffled discussions about whether or not it was feasible for Mum to leave her teaching position in order to pursue such a frivolous dream. A well-respected educator, Mum was heading down the road towards administration in the school system. But something different was calling her and she was brave enough to follow the path that really made her heart sing. She never went to work for the architect but the conversation and fork in the road led her to where she really wanted

to be – working with antiques. Antique dealers who lived passionately for their work, never stopping until the job was done. They instilled in all three children an attitude that anything and everything is possible in life if you really wanted to do something. My love of collectables, scrounging, antiques, putting things together and making them look beautiful must always be credited to my eccentric, passionate mother. I guess this very strong role model gave me courage and a can-do attitude when it came to creating our home in the French village of Bosgouet.

I had always loved cooking and entertaining and creating beautiful houses. Pete and I had bought our first tiny house in Melbourne and renovated it ourselves while we lived in it. Then we sold it and bought another old house. It was a pattern we have repeated throughout our married life. The houses were always in various states of disrepair, but Bosgouet was our biggest challenge yet. But here, in this peaceful, restorative corner of Normandy couldn't I recreate what I'd always done, just on a bigger scale? I could invite guests to my home, I could showcase the food of France, I could potter in jumble sales and brocantes and the fabric markets of Paris to create a completely immersive French experience for visitors. I knew that finally I had found a way to meld all my passions and make a living from it. And so The French Table was born. From May to September every year, for the past ten years, I have hosted people from all over the world. People who come for a taste of France. People who have their own French dream. An audible gasp is the usual response when guests arrive at Bosgouet. We like to think that the château's magic takes hold pretty quickly and makes guests feel welcomed and relaxed within minutes of arriving. There's a very special feeling at Bosgouet. She envelops you with her warmth and talks to you as if you are an old friend. She also has a magical way of making people open up and share like they never have before.

We lived in Bosgouet for two full years while we restored the château and established The French Table. Once it was up and running, we knew that we wanted to bring the children back to Australia. It was wonderful to return to the normality and the certainty of family and our home country. Little things meant life was so much easier. Of course the obvious advantage of speaking in English was a relief and made daily tasks so much simpler. When we first got home there was the ease of shopping at the supermarket where the checkout person actually packed your bag for you! ⤳ Although nothing had changed on the surface when we returned we had changed irreversibly. There were friendships that had gone by the wayside during our time away. Judgemental friends could not understand why we had done such a foolish thing as to pull four children out of school for an uncertain future in a foreign country. Unanswered emails, letters and Skype calls meant the end to friendships that we knew would never be resurrected. The children had similar experiences and we all found ourselves in the situation of working out who was true and worth the effort as we settled back in. ⤳ After that initial two years our lives took on a new pattern. During term one and two we lived at home in Melbourne as a family of six. In term three the older children would board at their schools and we would head off for The French Table season in France. Boarding school was not a concept I was familiar with and those were emotionally charged times for me. Pete had been a boarder from the age of 11 and assured me that our children were in the enviable position of having the best of both worlds! I often think that if I had looked ahead at the pain of separation back when we first bought the château it would never have happened. But I never thought about what we would do when the children were too old to spend the summer in France with us. I never asked myself how I would cope without my children for eight weeks until they could travel across for the school holidays. I sometimes think I must have been in a complete dream. The physical pain of that separation will never leave me as a mother. Each and every time I left the children I was rendered emotionally drained, and I would invariably arrive at the airport red-eyed, physically exhausted and racked with guilt! However, for all those agonies, I will forever be grateful for those first two years that we spent as a family in France. They brought us together in a way that I don't think would have been possible had we stayed in Melbourne. ❦

A FRENCH COLOUR PALETTE

A FRENCH COLOUR PALETTE

n France, grey is a much favoured country and city colour all on its own. Think of the shutters on Place Vendôme. I'm not talking about brutal mortar colour or concrete pavement grey here. This French grey is subtle and soft, with a blue or pink base. The colour is often used on painted furniture as well and gives it a wonderfully weighted feel. ✎ Grey teamed with creamy white is a very sophisticated and traditional Parisian palette and has always been popular in the French capital. It is common to see a white base used as a colour and not as a neutral. French whites are never cold, bright or fluorescent looking. Antique or clotted-cream matt whites are chosen, which have true warmth and layered depth. ✎ The French interpret colour very subtly and use it to tell a story, showing different hues at different times of the day. Paler colours are milky but still have depth. Strong colours are vibrant but never scream. ✎ Traditionally these beautiful French colours were very much dependant on a region's local colour pigments. When painting walls and furniture each region would use their local ingredients to mix pigments for the colour palette. Across France, traditional recipes for paint palettes included milky washes, lime washes and a greenish or grey-toned palette. When I think of the colour palette of Provence I imagine the olive groves, lavender fields and vineyards, and the enormous yellow sunflowers that turn their faces towards the brilliant Provence sun. ✎ Whether you choose to use a warm or cool palette remember that harmony is the key. Colours should not be in competition or shout rudely at each other. As the Impressionist painters in France discovered, time of day, weather and pure natural light play an immeasurable role in influencing decorative colour palettes. Always strive to create a harmony of complementary elegant tones to create the perfect French effect. ✎ After many trips to Place Vendôme in every light of the day Pete was finally happy with the French grey that was to become our new shutter colour. In the end a very helpful guard gave him a scraping of a shutter that was under renovation to take away for a perfect colour match! The shutters of Bosgouet were taken from their ancient hinges and immersed in an acid bath to remove all traces of the old, white flaking paint before the beautiful new grey – with the tiniest hint of blue – was applied. ✿

THE MANY INTERPRETATIONS
OF FRENCH BLUE.

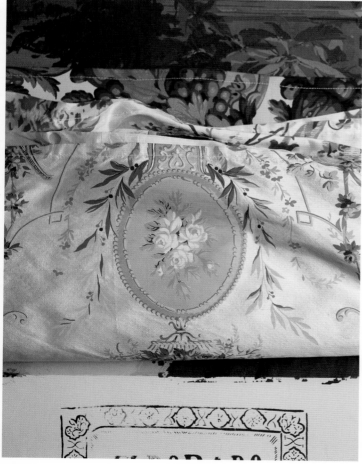

A FRENCH COLOUR PALLETE

Overleaf

MANY SHADES OF YELLOW
FEATURE IN OUR FRIENDS, TODD
AND AMY'S, LIVING ROOM.

A FRENCH COLOUR PALLETE

Opposite

THESE GORGEOUS CAST
IRON GATES WELCOME
VISITORS IN CAUMONT.

Above

I LOVE DOOR DETAILS.
ON OUR HONEYMOON IN
PARIS IN 1990 PETE TOOK
OVER TWENTY ROLLS OF
FILM JUST OF DOORS
AND DOOR DETAILS.

RECEPTION ROOMS

hen I first began to furnish Bosgouet I could often hear Mum talking to me. 'One room at a time, darling. Don't be ridiculous, of course you can do it!' Decorating a house can seem utterly daunting and there were many times that I didn't feel up to the task of properly preserving this historic property for future generations. In a way, I think we were fortunate that the house was in such disrepair when we moved in because we were able to slowly acquaint ourselves with every inch of her, to get a sense of her bones and her history, so when it came time to dress her we had had time to consider what we really wanted and what would suit the house. There's something very special about ancient houses. The patina, the wear, the feeling that one might get to the real soul of the house and its past inhabitants if you stop to listen carefully to what the house has to say. Château Bosgouet is of course a French house but when I arrived there I realised I had always lived in French-inspired homes. ❧

L'ENTRÉE

L'ENTRÉE

The first time I saw a château I thought of an expression that's perfect when talking about the entry to a house, 'We don't get a second chance at a first impression'. ✦ The design, placement and style of a house's entrance can have a strong effect on the look and feel of a home. When dreaming of my French house I knew that the entrance would be an important factor, a permanent welcome that I would see thousands of times over the coming years. I wanted it to be dramatic, as well as giving me that wonderful feeling of coming home. ✦ I remember very clearly the first time we drove along the winding driveway of Château Bosgouet in 2003. We couldn't see anything as we passed through the ancient iron gates. The majesty of the centuries-old trees was intoxicating and all encompassing as our car carefully took each curve of the road. Then, almost as if we had forgotten the reason we were there, the house came into view. At first we just had a glimpse through mottled sunlight and the majestic linden trees, and then we saw its exacting symmetry, grandeur, beauty and grace. It was spine-tingling knowing that somehow, some day she was going to be ours! ✦ There were three items on my list that were not negotiable when Pete and I set out to find the French home of our dreams — the divine and heavenly symmetry of French doors and windows, original Versailles parquetry flooring, and reception rooms with original moulding and plaster panelling. Everything else was up for discussion but those three elements were my absolute must haves! I guess I always look for good bones. By good bones I mean something I can work with. At first glance, it was the front steps of Bosgouet, and the heavy perfection of the cast-iron urns and planter boxes. The symmetry of the building with classic French windows was all I had ever dreamt of. I knew the house could be beautiful and shine again after years of neglect. ✦ When people enter your home you want them to remember the experience because it truly evokes your personal style. It might be the gorgeous heady aroma of gardenia flowers spilling over a front step, or a hall table always filled with beautiful flower arrangements. ✦ I love to decorate using collections and one of my favourites for the past thirty years has been blue and white china. I first started looking for it in my early twenties and before

Previous leaf
THE CHILDREN OF MY PARISIAN
FRIEND CARINA PEEKING
OUT ONTO THE GARDEN IN
THE LOIRE.

long I had accrued quite a large collection of ginger jars and platters. It's probably my favourite colour palette and is such a part of French-inspired living. I find blue and white timeless, fresh and calming. We saw it all over Paris on our honeymoon and it is always in favour. I am constantly changing my pieces around, grouping different ones together for a time before rearranging again. For many years my front entrance has displayed the ginger jars and a superb blue and white birdcage on a huge oak hunting table. Above hangs the enormous chandelier we commissioned a young artisan couple in Paris to make us in our first year at Château Bosgouet. ✕✦ It doesn't matter what story you want to tell at the entrance to your home as long as you tell it authentically. Make whatever impact you want but make sure it is true to those living there. ✕✦ Many Parisian apartments begin at the highly polished brass entrée security panel where the only way to peek beyond is to know the code. Tap the number and click, the weighted doors open. Step over the threshold, with the giant doors locking tight behind you – and you are in. Behind the solid oak of the Parisian entrance door lies another world. It's the secret world of the Parisian residence. A world of the grand courtyard entrée, panelled walls, ancient stoned floors and wrought-iron caged lifts flanked with elaborate stone stairs. Practicality meets pure elegance and intrigue in the Parisian apartment building. She is as important as the apartment itself. She is the prelude, the aperitif, and she sets the tone for what is to come. ✿

Opposite

THE ENTRÉE AT A FRIEND'S
16TH-CENTURY CHÂTEAU
NEAR LE BEC-HELLOUIN IN
NORMANDY.

PARQUETRY

PARQUETRY DESCRIBES THE USE OF BLOCKS OF WOOD arranged in a geometric pattern and is popular for both flooring and furniture. It was in Paris in the 1600s that the technique of parquetry flooring become accepted as French style. In a 1673 issue of Paris's most fashionable society magazine, *Mercure Galant*, it was explained to readers that 'people of quality' were forgoing dusty carpets in favour of parquetry throughout Paris. Although wooden plank flooring remained the norm in most homes, parquetry continued to be popular in grander homes throughout the 19th century. King Louis XIV's designers and architects created a special pattern specifically for the Palace of Versailles floors, which was composed of large squares of parquetry containing interlaced diagonal squares and laid on the bias. This parquetry was developed specifically to replace the marble flooring that required constant washing, and which had rotting joists beneath the floors at Versailles and at the Grand Trianon. This original pattern is still known as Parquet de Versailles and is the same pattern we have on the floors at Bosgouet. At the time parquetry first became popular, aristocrats all over France were having new parquetry patterns laid in their châteaux. These patterns are often still known by the name of the place where they were first installed. Practical and beautiful, parquetry floors are long lasting and require little or no maintenance. Even when pieces of parquetry become unstuck the offending blocks can simply be reglued. When we first arrived at Château Bosgouet we had a few areas where the parquetry needed replacing. Luckily for us we had a resident caretaker/gardener who was also very talented at restoring parquetry floors. A philosopher by night and talented parquetry restorer – among other things – by day! Today many designers like to replicate the grandeur of antique parquetry, either with reclaimed floors or wood, or using flooring companies that specialise in wood parquetry. It's a permanent and very expressive way to inject some pure French essence into your home. Back in 1999 Pete fell in love

A PERFECT EXAMPLE OF
VERSAILLES PARQUETRY.

with Château de la Ferté Frênel in the tiny Lower Normandy village of La Ferté Frênel. The pedigree of this historic monument is first class, with its prestigious staircase and great hall of marble. The Parisian architect Storès called on the painter/decorator Alphonse Ouri, who was once a student of Delacroix, to decorate the great hall, as well as the artist Godon to do the paintings that can be found within the *boiserie* panelling in the château's art and music salon. ➤ Numerous antique decorations, dating from before the construction of the castle, were brought by the Marquis Armand Alexis Odet De Montault, who inherited the domain in 1853. These antique and architectural decorations were brought from another château and included 18th-century Versailles-style parquetry, wainscoting from the end of the 17th century, and Louis XV and Louis XIV fireplaces. It is very high quality and very impressive. But for me, as much as I loved the château, the entrance, staircase and great hall lacked the warmth that I have come to love in many of these grand old houses. The floors and walls were all in an intricate heavy marble pattern, which I found cold and uninviting. I couldn't get past the fact the la Ferté Frênel did not have parquetry in the front entrance. There were parquetry rooms all over the château but I couldn't quite get this huge cold entrance, stairwell and great hall out of my mind, and I couldn't imagine transforming this vast space into an intimate family environment. ❧

GENEROUS CURTAINS
BILLOWING OVER PARQUETRY
FLOORS IS A CLASSIC
FRENCH LOOK.

L'ESCALIER

THE STAIRCASE IS NOT MERELY A WAY OF connecting the various levels of a house – it is the linchpin of a home. I have seen many examples that set a very French tone, from châteaux to farmhouses and everything in between. Made from stone or oak and in all sorts of designs, it is a space that can be both decorative and practical. ⤙ When we first moved into Château Bosgouet, the French-polished balustrade was in very bad condition, with the black ebony detail that ran through the middle missing in several places. My father and Pete scoured *brocante* shops, our workshop and local antique markets for replacement ebony. ⤙ The bullnose step is typically found at the bottom of the staircase and is semi-circular in shape. To make a truly dramatic French staircase, use stone for this first step. It's hard to beat for French elegance. Stripped-back oak or pine will also work beautifully, especially when waxed. Add a coloured runner for a classical tread treatment that will give your staircase a beautiful French tone. ⤙ Don't waste the space beneath the stairs. We have a tiny little French-tiled powder room under our main staircase. This space could also be used as a cellar or linen room. Or you could build a reading nook by adding simple banquette seating topped with gorgeous French fabric and covered cushions. Add a ruched lamp, some little gilded framed prints and voila! ⤙ I've always been a fan of wicker baskets strategically placed on the bottom step or halfway up the stairs. This is a wonderful way to organise laundry for upstairs bedrooms or when children's toys need to be packed away. Let's face it, it's easier for stuff to make its way down the stairs than it is for things to go up, and that can lead to a build-up of gadgets, toys, clothes and other paraphernalia overtaking your downstairs rooms. ⤙ If you have a landing halfway up the stairs, a lovely and very French note is to place one small wingback chair for a child, covered in something utterly delicious that you may not be brave enough to put en masse anywhere else. All you need to add is a little floor lamp and, if you have room, a tiny antique

A SIMPLE STAIRCASE AT A MANOR
IN THE LOIRE VALLEY WHERE
CONVERSATIONS AND GAMES
OFTEN HAPPEN.

Louis XVI-style marble-top *bouillotte* table, a small posy of flowers sitting in a cut-glass tumbler and a collection of books. I had this story halfway up the staircase in my house in Melbourne when the children were tiny. I would change their books regularly and keep the space beautiful in order to entice a little person to sit and read or just have some quiet time. I have given the main staircase at Bosgouet the same treatment, and often find a guest or member of the family perched there reading. ➤ The balustrade at Bosgouet was one of the very first projects Dad worked on for us. We never asked him to do anything at the château – just enjoy himself, read, eat dinner with us every night and have a lovely time making new friends while being immersed in the French countryside. But Dad being Dad he wanted projects and loved to feel needed. One day we found him working away on the baluster (the plain or decorative pillar that forms part of a series to support a rail) on the main staircase. These balusters are iron and very decorative and Dad was busy polishing them with a soft steel wool pad. He loved this sort of project, which allowed him to work away at his own pace and that, once completed, gave great satisfaction and pure joy to all of us. ➤ He went on to paint each riser – the vertical section that runs between the horizontal treads of the staircase. Each one was carefully painted in a jet-black sheen, which set off the French oak parquetry treads exquisitely. He sanded the treads carefully by hand and then nourished them with a combination of turpentine and linseed oil until the wood came back to life. It's now one of the first jobs I do every spring at Bosgouet. ➤ In the spring of 2013 we came back to the château to find that Dad had renovated the entire west tower spiral staircase, explaining that 'I just did a couple of steps each day'. It was typical of Dad to make so little of a job that I imagine took hundreds of hours. At the end of that summer Dad passed away very unexpectedly and there at the top of that spiral staircase was his little pot of wax and soft steel wool. As we don't really use that staircase it still sits there waiting for Dad to return and rub a little more love and attention back into the oak treads of the Bosgouet stairs. I know I'll have to move it one day but not yet … not yet. ❦

Below

STAIRCASE DETAIL OF
OUR FRIEND TODD HASE'S
BEAUTIFULLY RESTORED
CHÂTEAU.

Opposite

CLASSIC OAK TREADS GRACE
THIS BEAUTIFUL STAIRCASE
IN NORMANDY, WHICH IS
DOMINATED BY CAST-IRON
BALUSTRADING.

LE
SALON

LE SALON

A passion for elegance is at the very heart of every living space I create, and is inspired by the French *joie de vie*. This inspiration comes in many forms. I have found that the best French interiors showcase a range of influences. It could be travel, history, poetry, art – whatever affects our lives. My personal philosphy when decorating in the French style is that first and foremost the space, especially a sitting room, must be liveable. I believe in buying impeccable quality and investing in very special pieces that will anchor the room and give it sophistication and authenticity. This is the way we give a room a soul. I adore those immaculate French rooms that are put together with precision and history, and where the furnishings match the period of the house. But I cannot live with them. The formality and rigidness of tiny, upright gilded chairs does not lend itself to the modern and relaxed way in which we live. For my sitting room, I've always chosen oversized couches that look luxurious and are a haven on a cold Sunday afternoon, when the sun filters through the windows and the family is sitting and playing around me. I love to be surrounded by collections and colour that speak volumes about the personalities that make up our home. There is always a large silver tray piled with cups and saucers, sugar, creamer and a large white porcelain teapot. And stacks of books on French art, architecture, homes, gardens, travel and antiques that say so much about our interests and passions. When planning your living space, choose colours that you love and don't hesitate to be bold and brave. Look at your wardrobe for inspiration. What are you drawn to? Someone once said to me that every room should have a splash of red in it. It could be a group of accent cushions or a new piece of artwork. A juxtaposition of richly textured materials will add dimension so combine smooth linens with more heavily textured brocades, and mix varied woods with marble. It's this sort of diverse palette of fabrics, patterns and organic pieces that give a space soul and depth, and make for a truly French chic home!

Opposite
I LOVE THE AUTHENTICITY OF THIS TAPESTRY AND COULDN'T BEAR TO SEE THIS PIECE REUPHOLSTERED. IT'S SUCH A TALKING POINT AT THIS BEAUTIFUL CHÂTEAU ON THE SEINE.

Overleaf
SIMPLE YET CLASSICAL FRENCH LINES ABOUND IN THIS 16TH-CENTURY CHÂTEAU BELONGING TO OUR FRIENDS THE WALKERS.

THE FIRST TIME I ENTERED
THIS GRAND SALON
BELONGING TO OUR FRIENDS
NICK AND IREIDE I AUDIBLY
GASPED. IT IS SO AUTHENTIC
AND TRUE TO ITS
16TH-CENTURY BONES.

Overleaf

THIS IS A BEAUTIFUL 8TH-ARRONDISSEMENT
APARTMENT WHERE WE HAVE SPENT FAMILY TIME
OVER THE YEARS. THE HERO PIECE IN THIS STUDY
THAT DOUBLES AS A THIRD BEDROOM IS THE
BAROMETER THAT SITS DOMINATING THE ROOM.

LE SALON

Above

A MODERN SOFA AND COLOUR
FEATURE IN THIS 16TH-CENTURY
COLOMBAGE FARMHOUSE.

Opposite

A HEAVENLY SCENE AT FERME
ST SIMEON IN HONFLEUR
FEATURING OAK PANELLING, TAUPE
UPHOLSTERY AND WHITE FLORAL
ARRANGEMENTS.

I LOVE THE BEAMS AND THE RAW
BRICK WALLS IN LINDA AND
JOHN'S HOUSE.

FRENCH
PANELLING

THE FIRST TIME I EVER HEARD THE WORD 'BOISERIE'
was in 1997. We were visiting our first château – a gorgeous soft-yellow
stone mansion that was built in the 17th century – 20 kilometres east of the
town of Fontainebleau. The day was icy with a top temperature of minus
three degrees so it was with haste that Pete and I and our then three young
children shuffled inside hoping that the heating would be on. The interior
of the château was room after room of *boiserie* wall panelling painted
a soft yellow hue. Weeks later and after many châteaux inspections,
I realised that the *boiserie* of that château near Fontainebleau had set me
up for disappointment, time and time again, as I entered homes without this
wonderful treatment. *Boiserie* is the term used to describe ornate or
intricately designed wood panelling. The earliest examples were unpainted
but later it was popular to paint these beautiful mouldings and also gild
them. Our gilded sitting room at Château Bosgouet is a beautiful example
of *boiserie*, and has been painted in a muted grey lime-washed palette with
gilded edges. We have touched up damaged sections but will never totally
paint over the French grey or the original gilding as it is this patina that
makes it so alluring and extra special.

FRENCH *BOISERIE* AND
SILK-EMBOSSED CURTAINS
ARE CLASSICALLY BEAUTIFUL
WITH A BRASS TIE-BACK IN
AN APARTMENT IN THE
6TH ARRONDISSEMENT.

Well-designed or original wall panelling can bring a scale and proportion to a room or create a mood that cannot be obtained quite as successfully in any other way. From a purely practical perspective *boiserie* can also incorporate concealed storage or even a secret door, as is so often the case in French châteaux. ⌒ Traditionally, *boiserie* panels are not just confined to the walls of a room but used to decorate doors and cupboards, and frame French windows and shelves. *Boiserie* can often include oil paintings or pictures, with the carving framing the picture rather like a conventional frame. Historically these beautiful and intricate wall panels were handcarved out of wood, which was possible in the 1700s when labour was cheap. These days, if you are really keen for a touch of *boiserie* in your home, then a trip to France to scour the antique markets is a must! ⌒ Parisian apartments and the Palace of Versailles are my picks to enjoy inspiration and fine examples of *boiserie*. I could sit for hours admiring its intricacy and the way it frames and anchors a room, defining and demanding a respect that no other treatment can expect. ⌒ If you wanted to incorporate a little *boiserie* into your own home you can often pick up pieces of panelling at Les Puces. One guest at Bosgouet bought three gorgeous panels from one of my local antique haunts and had them shipped back to Sydney to incorporate into her new powder room. She was smitten with the *boiserie* and said she would leave it in its original state. It was a gorgeous washed-out sage green. Another guest bought a glorious example of *boiserie* at the annual Les Puces de Deauville, a wonderful three-day event that occurs in the impossibly beautiful seaside resort town of Deauville every year in May. ❦

Above

DEEP FEATHER COUCHES
UPHOLSTERED IN EGG YOLK
SILK DOMINATE
THIS 16TH-CENTURY
CHÂTEAU. I LOVE WATCHING
MY FRIEND LINDA PUNCH
AND PUFF THE CUSHIONS.

RECEPTION ROOMS

UPHOLSTERED
WALLS

THERE'S SOMETHING EXTRAORDINARY AND LUXURIOUS but also very warm and inviting about a room with upholstered walls, and it's not just the visual stimulation. The first time I walked into a room with upholstered walls I immediately noticed the difference in sound, or rather the lack of it. People's speech was quieter and that hollow echo that sometimes fills a room was absent, resulting in an intimate, relaxed experience. The French have been upholstering walls and doing it exquisitely for centuries. Wall upholstery evolved from early medieval times when huge hung tapestries helped keep cold winter draughts at bay. Fixed wall upholstery was introduced in the 17th century when opulent fabrics became more readily available. By the 18th century the nobility were using silk wall hangings. Over the years wall upholstery has evolved through various techniques. In the earliest days tapestries were simply hung on walls. After the Renaissance, the selected fabric was stretched and fixed with tacks onto ornamental wooden frames lining the walls inside each room of châteaux and the grander *manoir* houses. Artisan wall upholsterers used to hold tacks in their mouths, which allowed them to grip the fabric with the other hand. Of course this wasn't good for the teeth or the stomach when the tiny tacks were accidentally swallowed!

My first real experience with wall upholstery was at the château of Todd Hase, an inspiring New York City and Florida interior designer, who had renovated and decorated the château from top to toe. Situated just ten minutes' drive from Château Bosgouet, we were taken on a tour of the house and I had to stop myself touching every wall in the beautiful residence. I remember so well entering the first room at the château. The entire salon was fitted with a sea blue-green striped fabric with a donkey-coloured background. The chatter from the guests in other rooms and the thumping feet of scampering children running up staircases did not disturb us. Upholstered walls are great soundproofing! ⤜ Wall upholstery is a long-term decorating feature because of its high cost so it's a good idea to upholster a tiny room or just a feature wall and see if you like it. A classic stripe that won't date is a great way to start and gives a room a perfect foil for a French-inspired colour palette. ✿

Opposite
A ROOM CAN HAVE A
WONDERFULLY TEXTURED FEEL
WITH LAYERS OF UPHOLSTERY:
ON THE WALLS, IN CURTAINS
AND AS LAMPSHADES.

Overleaf
RUCHED SILK WALLS LINE THIS
LIBRARY/SALON AT L'HOTEL IN
PARIS. THIS PARISIAN SECRET
WAS OSCAR WILDE'S LAST HOME
AND HAS BEEN COMPLETELY
REMODELLED BY PARISIAN
DESIGNER JACQUES GARCIA.

TRUMEAU AND GILDED MIRRORS

THE FIRST TIME WE VISITED CHATEAU BOSGOUET I really did not know what to expect. I don't recall if I had even looked at the *fiche* – the document that described the property. As I walked through her doors that day in 2003, I started to tick off my must haves. Versailles oak parquetry flooring. Tick! French windows in perfect symmetry. Tick, tick! Three big reception rooms with original moulding and plaster panelling. Tick, tick, tick! ⤙ I peeked around a huge pair of panelled doors off the back entrance on the reception level. And there was the most delicious mirror sitting nonchalantly above the fireplace in what I imagined might have been a small bedroom or a library. The real estate agent told me that it was a Trumeau mirror. I had no idea what this meant but he explained that these gilded mirrors were originally manufactured in France in the 18th century. 'This decorative art form of unrivalled quality has long been praised as the epitome of elegance and the finest of craftsmanship and you have three fine examples here at Château Bosgouet.' He went on to say that a typical centrepiece of an 18th-century château interior was the Trumeau mirror. A long mirror set into panelling and topped with a painting or carved motif, it was both decorative and functional. ⤙ Most antique gilded mirrors are very ornate. What differentiates Trumeau mirrors from other mirrors is the decorative portion at the top. Their larger size means that they can

A GILDED MIRROR SITS ON
A SIDE TABLE IN THE SALON
IN A CHÂTEAU NEAR
LE BEC-HELLOUIN,
DEEP IN RURAL NORMANDY.

be displayed on their own or over a piece of furniture. They are not only a mirror but also a unique piece of art and almost always rectangular. Those designed to be placed above a mantelpiece, rather than between windows, can have candles placed in front of the mirror to increase ambient light. ⤚ Historically the gilded mirror was always hung on walls although these days you will often see them simply leaning against a wall. They have become highly sought after as attractive additions to homes the world over and add a unique French note. I often see gilded mirrors in rural *brocante* shops and have started collecting them in earnest. I've never seen one that wasn't exquisite in its intricate detail. ⤚ Many people look to professionals to buy for them but trust me – once you have a handle on where to go and how to haggle – you will be hooked and able to negotiate your own French purchases. I've watched a couple with no French language skills negotiate a price, shipping and a few cadeaux – free gifts – after two days of antiquing with me through the French countryside. They have been back to France now several times and returned to the dealers, antique markets and annual *brocante* shops I introduced them to. They love their new hobby and travel almost exclusively now to shop for special pieces they can take back to their Australian home. ❧

HANGING ART

THE ART OF HANGING PICTURES IS A BALANCING ACT of spacing, colour palettes and getting the relationship between pictures just right. A gallery curator or interior designer will say that the way art is displayed is crucial and can be totally transformative or a complete disaster. ✎ The beautiful and very French style of hanging numerous pieces of art all over a wall is called 'salon style'. It originated in 1667 at the first official art exhibition of the Académie des Beaux-Arts in Paris. Between 1748 and 1890 this exhibition was arguably the greatest annual or biennial art event in the Western world. Salon style is a wonderfully attractive option because the viewer focuses on the collective effect rather than individual pieces. I particularly love this style above a prominent piece of furniture such as a beautiful settee or hall table in a salon or front entrance. It gives real depth to a room. It works well when there is a combination of different mediums – oil paintings, sketches, prints, photographs or etchings – and frames in different styles and sizes. This sort of mix has a French charm, as well as providing an anchor point for the space. I don't believe in waiting until there is enough money to buy original artworks. Postcards, posters, children's drawings or pages taken from books can look equally special when framed and arranged in this way. ✎ Here's a good tip someone gave me early on when hanging art in a salon style. Place your pictures on the floor in different configurations. I like to leave them on the ground for a couple of days while I contemplate the hang. Aim for one central piece, progressing from large to small pieces as you move outwards. For a salon hang, keep them fairly close together. I work on 3 centimetres between pictures. ✎ Hang artwork or mirrors with a view to proportion and balance. If, for example, you are hanging a mirror or picture over a fireplace never leave too much space under the piece. People often make the mistake of hanging art too high on the wall. Pete always uses a spirit level to make sure pictures, paintings, photographs and mirrors are straight, but in the

A FRIEND IN THE LOIRE VALLEY HANGS SOME FRAMES WITHOUT PICTURES, WHICH ADDS INTRIGUE TO A WALL SPACE.

end you should always stand back and trust your eye. Walls are not always level, particularly in period homes. ➤ I was inspired many years ago to begin an art collection. It started with one of my weekly visits to a favourite auction house where I found myself up in the art room looking at paintings in gilded frames that might adorn the many blank walls of my home. Since that time and that first purchase – a very grim gentleman in a huge gilded frame – we have bought many pieces of artwork. That chance climb of the stairs at Leonard Joel in Melbourne has led to a keen interest in art and a personal collection based purely on what I think I will like looking at on the walls of Château Bosgouet and at home in Melbourne. Everyday scenes and beautiful landscapes are typical of the French art I have collected over the years, although I must confess that I have often been attracted to the frame first. After all, what says French style like the gilded frame of a painting or a mirror? It can become the absolute centrepiece of a room. ➤ I don't follow any guidelines for buying pieces but I do have one fundamental rule. I only buy what I love. I have an insatiable love of the Impressionists and, while I can hardly have a Monet, Manet or Renoir, that period has certainly influenced my buying. I remember purchasing a wonderful scene of a forest floor that was very much in the style of the Impressionists, with its short brush strokes and dappled light. This work adorned our family home in Australia for a decade before being transported to Bosgouet. I can't tell you how many of our French friends have admired this piece. ➤ Collecting is a great way to learn about the art world and makes a wonderful hobby. Auctions, both local and online, provide an opportunity to look closely at anything of interest. However, at an auction it is easy to feel intimidated or get swept away and end up paying a lot more than you intended. Many years ago, when I was still a teenager, my parents taught me how to bid at an auction. They also advised me to leave absentee bids, which meant that I would keep to my spending limit. An auction house with good credentials and reputation will never take the highest absentee bid if there are no other bids. I've had remarkable luck over the years leaving absentee bids and it's always thrilling to get a text or an email announcing that I have been successful. Of course, there is a great thrill in attending and bidding in person once you can trust yourself not to get completely carried away. ❀

SALON STYLE HANGINGS ARE
MOST EFFECTIVE WHEN ALL
THE ART IS OF A TYPE. IN THIS
INSTANCE BLACK-AND-WHITE
ENGRAVINGS.

Opposite
ONE WAY TO INSTANTLY ADD
ELEGANCE, SOPHISTICATION
AND A CLASSICAL FRENCH
TOUCH TO ANY ROOM IS TO
INTRODUCE A BUST INTO
YOUR DÉCOR. THEY CAN
BE FOUND THROUGHOUT
MY FRIEND JULIETTE'S
APARTMENT.

HANGING ART

115

LA SALLE À MANGER

LA SALLE À MANGER

The art of the table and all that goes with that exquisite beauty belongs first and foremost to France where the luxury and detail of the French aristocracy lives on in *la salle à manger*. ✾ There are so many delightful ways to bring a French sensibility to the dining room. It doesn't matter if your dining room is grand or small, or whether you want a very formal French look or a rustic country look. Antique and flea markets are ideal places to purchase unique furniture for your dining room. And if the piece doesn't match an overall interior design, it can easily be reupholstered or stripped back and repolished. ✾ A dining room furnished in the French style could pair a thickly topped wooden provincial table with a delicately carved sideboard bearing motifs of fruit and flora, both equally at home in the room. French country rustic farmhouse furniture can be combined with elegant Empire pieces and a majestic Norman wedding armoire. Painted finishes can be mixed with toile, pottery and copper – a look that's distinctively French. ✾ I have such a strong memory of dinner in a gorgeous Haussmann apartment in the 1st arrondissement of Paris, decorated in a French style that will never go out of fashion. Our hostess Clotilde had used a rich royal blue as a wall colour for her *salle à manger*. She had picked out white for crown and trim moulding, giving the immediate feel of French style. The room was furnished in rich textiles, crystal chandeliers, carved furniture and exquisitely layered curtains. It was enhanced by the backdrop of the Arc de Triumph, beautifully lit on that cold December night, which could be seen through their beautiful French windows. These windows were dressed with heavy curtains billowing all over the Versailles parquetry floor. They were made of heavy silk boarded with embossed trim and tied back with exquisitely made tassels. ✾ There was an ornamental centrepiece displayed on the formal dining table. I commented on its beauty and our host Jean Françoise explained that it was called a *surtout de table*, which had evolved from a simple plate or bowl on which to stand candlesticks and condiments. He said that it had often taken the form of a long narrow tray made of precious or gilded metals, sometimes made in sections to allow its length to be determined by the leaves added to the table. Since that day I have seen many examples, as they are still used in the most formal dining rooms. ✍ During the latter half of the 18th century and throughout the 19th century, no formal French table was considered complete without a *surtout de table*. One notable example, commissioned by Napoleon III, was made by Christofle in 1852 and used at state banquets in the Tuileries Palace. When the palace caught fire in 1871, it was rescued from the smoking debris and is now on display at the *Musée des Arts Décoratifs* in Paris. ✍ Another French touch I saw at Clotilde and Jean Françoise's home was the *porte-couteaux* or knife rests. They were first seen and used in early 18th-century households in France and were invented to save the tablecloth from being soiled by cooking juices. They came in sets and were often made of costly materials such as gold, silver, mother of pearl and ivory. The French popularised these knife rests and continue to use them today. They are a very collectable little item and I often see them in antique markets and *brocante* shops. Many guests who have visited Château Bosgouet over the years have purchased *porte-couteaux*. It's the perfect souvenir for those wanting to take a little piece of France home and for their French-style *salle à manger*. It's also very practical. Imagine the new-found freedom of using one knife and fork for all courses! ✍ Another useful French invention that I've been collecting for some years now is a *manche à gigot*. It's a leg-of-lamb holder, although I've also seen it used to hold a leg of ham. It secures the leg while carving, and is a truly beautiful and practical tool for the serious Francophile. Again these gorgeous little gadgets are often found at *brocante* shops and at the Paris flea markets as they are a common household item in France and have been since the early 18th century. ✍ Crystal decanters are another easy way to inject a French story into your dining room. Keep them sparkling clean by filling the decanter with white vinegar; leave overnight and flush with cool water. ✍ I also have a couple of wonderful absinthe fountains. Absinthe became very popular in France in the late 18th century. The Green Fairy (*le fée verte*), as it is commonly referred to, originated in the canton of Neuchâtel in Switzerland. The fountains make an incredible talking piece in any *salle à manger* and evoke lively conversation. Absinthe spoons are very collectible as well. They are beautifully decorated and perforated slotted spoons that are used

to dissolve a cube of sugar in a glass of absinthe. The spoon is usually flat, with a notch in the handle where it rests on the rim of the glass. Team the spoons with a set of absinthe glasses. And of course you can buy a bottle of absinthe and add it to your other liquors. It could result in a very interesting dinner party! A collection of vintage absinthe posters can also make great artwork in a more informal dining room. ❦

Opposite
JULIE'S TABLE IN THE LOIRE – A NEW FRIEND WHO INVITED ME TO HER TABLE AFTER 'MEETING' ON INSTAGRAM!

Overleaf
I HAVE LOVED THIS DINING ROOM WITH ITS ZUBER *LES VUES DU BRÉSIL (1829)* WALLPAPER SINCE I FIRST SAW IT. IT'S ALWAYS SUCH A PRIVILEGE TO BE INVITED TO DINE AT THIS BEAUTIFUL CHÂTEAU ON THE SEINE.

LA SALLE À MANGER

121

Opposite

WE TOOK MELBOURNE
FRIENDS JANE AND STEPHEN
TO AN ANNUAL PARTY AT THIS
CHÂTEAU IN THE TINY HAMLET
OF JONQUAY AND THEY
ENDED UP BUYING IT.

Below

A COOL PLACE TO SIT ON A
HOT SUMMER'S DAY – A CELLAR
NEAR HARCOURT.

Opposite
THE HASE FAMILY LOVE TO
ENTERTAIN AND THE ANNUAL
FETE FOR DAUGHTERS CHLOE
AND AVA IS ALWAYS A MUCH-
ANTICIPATED EVENT, WITH
PRETTY PASTEL VIGNETTES
ALWAYS GREETING GUESTS.

Below
CHINA COLLECTIONS ARE
PART AND PARCEL OF FRENCH
COUNTRY LIVING.

CHANDELIERS

THE WORD 'CHANDELIER' ORIGINATES FROM THE French word *chandelle*, which means candle holder. When the chandelier first appeared in the 14th century that was exactly what a chandelier was – a simple candle holder. The original chandeliers consisted of two wooden pieces forming a cross with a spike at the end of each piece of wood to hold or push a candle into. Due to their cost only the wealthy could afford to own and use them, and they were mainly found inside churches, abbeys and other large gathering places. The Industrial Revolution in 1760 brought a changed world and with these changes came opportunities for people who had not been able to afford such luxuries in the past. *Les arts décoratifs* – ornate decorative objects that had once only been available to the wealthy – were now available to many more people. A middle class was emerging and they were showing off their new prosperity with beautiful decorations like chandeliers. They began to team the true grandeur that had once been only for the aristocracy with the elegance of the French Empire chandelier. This classic French form of lighting made of gilded brass or wrought iron adorned salons all over Paris. The iron components of the chandelier were combined with shimmering drops of crystal that provided the salons of the new middle class with glamour and style. French chandeliers are typically made of brass or iron that is often hand-crafted in a curve. This curve encases and frames the light they capture.

Pure and unadulterated elegance and drama is what the chandelier brings to the French-inspired home. Look for your own French Empire centrepiece when next in Paris. The flea markets at Clignancourt are a great place to start. You will pay a fraction of the price that you will pay at home from a dealer or interior designer and an original French Empire chandelier will provide you with a lifetime of enduring allure. ⤜ I've always lived with chandeliers. As a child Mum had them hung in our suburban home, insisting they were kept spotlessly clean at all times. I remember Dad up a ladder carefully polishing each crystal with a rag in one hand and a bottle of glass cleaner in the other! Mum said to me once that 'one of the easiest and most expressive ways to capture and add a French essence to a room is by adding a show-off. The piece that demands complete attention as soon as someone enters that room.' I think this sage advice has always been with me intuitively and I find using a chandelier as the centre of attention works so well. It exudes French flavour and gives a room an instant anchor. ✤

A TWINKLING CHANDELIER
DOMINATES A FRIEND'S SALON.

TOILE

TOILE IS DISTINCTLY FRENCH IN DESIGN AND BRINGS
a French sensibility to any home. Used to upholster furniture and walls as well
as make curtains, toile has been a mainstay of French style for generations.
My favourite colour combinations in toile are grey and raspberry, raspberry
and clotted cream, and blue and yolk. I am particularly enamoured with
antique versions of toile and love to hunt them out at *brocantes*. We drove
up to Paris early one Friday morning with the intention of spending all day
in the 18th arrondissement. Our objective was simple. Find an early morning
park in Montmartre and a bar or bistro where we could have a good
omelette and coffee and then explore every inch of this quarter looking
for the elusive new fabric for the dining room chairs at Château Bosgouet.
We knew that this charming – some might say grungy – neighbourhood
can be touristy, but there are treasures to discover in the surrounding
streets if you take the time to look. ➤➤ In the mid-18th century, toile
was inspired by the fabrics found in the East and Asia depicting themes of
the 'new world'. These fabrics were first printed using engraved wooden
plates, and later engraved copper rolls in the town of Jouy-en-Josas,
just south of Versailles. The raw cloth was washed in the River Bievre,
a 36-kilometre river that flows into the River Seine. The natural chemical
make-up of the river water gave the material its distinctive off-white
background. The fabric was then left to dry in the fields around the town
before being printed with a one-colour design. Traditionally the toile fabrics
were printed in red and purple and later in pink and light blue. It became
commonly known as the *toile de Jouy* because of its town of origin. ➤➤
Competition within the textile industry was intense in 18th-century France.
Christophe-Phillipe Oberkampf's factory in Jouy-en-Josas originated some
of the first toile – a French word meaning 'linen cloth'. Collaborating
with his long-term designer, Jean Baptiste Huet, Oberkampf was able to
differentiate himself from his major competitors through his extraordinary,

BEAUTIFUL TOILE
IN EARTHY TONES.

elaborate designs and intricate stories and depictions of everyday France. By the end of his life, he had created a unique French national aesthetic that was loved all over the world, with more than 30,000 trademarked designs in his textile collection. Since that time, the appeal of toile has never faltered. ✐ Oberkampf and Huet lived through multiple royal ascensions. There was never any doubt about their skill at textile manufacturing but history suggests that they were also very adept at swiftly disassociating themselves from their most famous patrons – namely Napoleon and Louis XVIII. It's amazing that Oberkampf and Huet kept their heads throughout the barbaric days of the Revolution. But, like their beautiful pastoral-scene fabric they never seemed to go out of favour. ✐ Toile also became a political tool of sorts with its artistic representations of grand civic events. On one early print, '*La Ballon de Gonesse*', Huet depicts Jacques Charles and Nicolas Marie-Noel Robert as they ride a hot air balloon over the Tuileries Garden. This image was particularly suited to textile and became typical of the type of image used. The design not only showcased France's scientific advancements but also seemed to capture the social and spiritual aspirations of the French. The French landscape is rendered in romantic and bucolic styles. Other designs showed scenes of France's alliance with America and other far away places such as Jerusalem and Egypt, creating experiences of early armchair travel and endless opportunity for imagining and daydreaming. ❦

A SELECTION OF TOILES,
INCLUDING THE RASPBERRY
AND GREY TOILE OF MY
DINING ROOMS CHAIRS
(BOTTOM RIGHT).

TASSELS

TASSELS HAVE DEFINITELY COME A LONG WAY from being a simple knot to a decorative addition. The tassel was around in biblical times when they were used on garments and heavier items such as blankets and camel rugs. They have been found in the ancient tombs of the pharaohs. From the simplistic tassel designs of the Renaissance to a slightly larger but more formal appearance during the Empire period, and then through to the extravagance and opulence of the Victorian era, the tassel of today pays homage to many periods in history. ⤝ The word 'tassel' originates from the Latin word *tassau* meaning clasp. It was simply a weaving knot that was used to tie off various clothing and fabrics to prevent unravelling. When this becomes a series of threads wound around a suspended string the result can be given any curvature, which is how the tassel became stylised. ⤝ It is the French who are credited with the real evolution of the tassel into ornamentation. In the 18th century in France all the best dressed curtains, sofas and armoires were garnished with decorative tassels made of cotton, wool or silk. There were large ones and small ones, some incredibly elaborate and others very plain. The sole purpose of *passementerie* – tassels, fringes, braid, beading – was to add a magical, whimsical dash of colour! ⤝ The tassel has become a functional and decorative object that never seems to go out of fashion, and is synonymous with France and French design. Today, artisans all over the world are creating tassels of great beauty and detail, with some fetching thousands for a single hand-made creation. When matched with fabric, *passementerie* gives an incomparable touch to any room. An ornate tie-back over a curtain, a sofa fringe, or braid or gimp for cushions can enhance, contrast or complement a dominant colour while adding delicate refinement. ⤝ Since the 16th century, when the first Guild of the *Passementiers* was established and the art of *passementerie* began, the practitioners have had to do a seven-year apprenticeship in order to become a master of the guild.

BILLOWING SILK CURTAINS
GARNISHED WITH A LARGE
ORNATE GOLD TASSEL.

Seven years! I wonder if the fact that it takes this long gets to the real heart of why French style is revered and copied the world over. No wonder the French look for truly beautiful craftsmanship in every aspect of their lives. >•••• Traditional silk tassels with corded tops and fringed skirts are still made by such companies as Declercq, which supplies the great decorators of the world with custom-made work. Since the 1850s they have been making exquisite tassels with old looms and *passementiers*. It is a family business, now in its sixth generation. >•••• About 80 per cent of the work at Declercq is done completely by hand, and some of the looms date from the late 19th century. The Declercq showroom in Paris is well worth visiting. It is a mini-museum displaying their historic work and is open to the public. ❦

ROOMS FOR RETREAT

The large French country house tends to be a collection of very distinct separate living spaces rather than the open-plan living that you might typically see in modern homes or renovated inner-city dwellings elsewhere. The French home stays true to its original nature with a very separate salon, *salle à manger* and so on. Although some people do renovate and open rooms up, I have to say for the most part I have not seen this in any of my friends' homes in Normandy. At Bosgouet it is still possible to achieve that feeling of open-plan living, especially on the reception room level, as the sheer size of the rooms gives a feeling of open plan. When the double doors are flung back between the entrée and the dining room, and the salon and the entrée, there is certainly a liaison between the rooms that feels familiar to a modern sensibility. There is also a small, enclosed kitchen and a separate utility room on this floor. I have often looked at one of the huge salons at Bosgouet and imagined a purpose-built open-plan kitchen – a practical space for all to gather – but then remind myself that this is a French château with her own charm and nature that cannot, and should not, be dragged into a period that her old bones do not understand. The heart and soul of an old French country house, in my opinion, must be respected so as not to disturb the perfect balance of the architecture and period.

LA
BIBLIOTHÈQUE

LA BIBLIOTHÈQUE

or as long as I can remember I have loved to curl up on a chair and read, flick through a big coffee table book or delve into a new recipe book. If you're an avid fan of retreating to a quiet, relaxing space to get away from the world then a library might be just right for your French-inspired home. In the past, libraries have had a reputation of being an extra rather than the norm. Today, home libraries are becoming more popular, often with home offices sharing the space. You don't have to have a large mansion or a French château, or even a dedicated room to achieve a beautiful library. ✒ At a delightful *manoir* in the Loire Valley my friend Julie has created a lovely library nook with the help of Belgian interior designer, David Neothissen. They chose a colour from the palette of hunter greens, which is dark and rich. Today's home libraries can be light and bright or furnished in a deep-coloured traditional décor. It all depends on what colours complement you and your lifestyle. ✒ At Château Bosgouet I chose a small room on the reception level that doubles as a tiny extra guest room. I've often found one of the children there lying on the oak sleigh bed reading, sleeping or listening through their headphones. This little room is situated right next to the French doors that lead on to the back terrace. It is an ideal library as it can be shut off from the world, offering a sanctuary where the reader can completely unwind and escape the pressures of everyday life. ✒ One of the first things to do when developing a home library is to determine how many books you have. The library should be able to hold all the books you own. So, assess your storage needs and decide if bookshelves from floor to ceiling are necessary. A practical and very French look is to use the space over the top of a doorway as a bonus area for storage. If you have a smaller collection, consider using open shelving for a modern touch or signature pieces of furniture that can hold different collections of books. ✒ If you plan on combining your library with your home office, make sure you assess what is needed for both functions. If you need to incorporate a computer, telephone, printer and so on then this may be another great place to have an armoire. ✒ Make sure when you are creating this lovely space for reading, working and dreaming that you install proper lighting. Ideally the natural light will be

Previous leaf

SYMMETRY AND STUNNING
FRENCH MOULDING ABOUND
IN THIS DELICIOUS APARTMENT
CLOSE TO THE LUXEMBOURG
GARDENS IN PARIS.

sufficient for reading and working in the daytime. I love using side table lamps in the evenings, often in combination with accent lighting for artwork displayed on the walls. Gilded wall sconces look beautiful in home libraries and give an added sense of French authenticity to a project. They can also look very stylish attached to bookshelves as ambient lighting. ⤨ If you are in Paris and would like to add to your library collection, go to Librairie Galignani. Situated on Rue de Rivoli, Librairie Galignani is, according to its impressive history, the oldest English-language bookshop on the European continent. It also happens to be the most elegant. This independent bookstore has been run by six generations of the Galignani family and has been a landmark since 1801. It is a home away from home for English-speaking visitors and expats living in the French capital. ⤨ Librairie Galignani moved to 224 Rue de Rivoli in 1856, where it stands majestically underneath its massive arches and imposing arcade, flanked by the Hotel Le Meurice and Angelina's Salon de Thé. It has witnessed many important historical events and welcomed countless famous visitors. The books are not just mere products to be sold but precious objects of 'wisdom and aesthetic delight' according to the current owner, Danielle Cillien Sabatier. 'Bookselling is not just an ordinary business, but a mission and a family tradition lasting more than two hundred years.' ⤨ The French-polished wooden shelves that were manufactured in the 1930s hold an impressive collection of around 50,000 titles. Besides the selection of English titles (divided into fiction, politics and history), there is an incredible fine arts department, which can satisfy even the most demanding art expert. The knowledgeable staff are known for their ability to fulfil the oddest literary requests, so if there's a book you can't find anywhere you know where to turn. Librairie Galignani is also famous for the literary events it holds every month and their monthly newsletters and invitations to special events are sent all over the world. I always know there will be a pile of Galignani books under the Christmas tree each year from Pete to me. ❦

Opposite

THIS LIBRARY NOOK IS THE
PERFECT PLACE TO RETREAT.

Above

ANYWHERE CAN BECOME
A SPACE FOR ONESELF.
ALL YOU NEED IS A SMALL
DESK, A CHAIR AND A LITTLE
IMAGINATION. A PERFECT
PLACE TO READ, WORK
OR CREATE.

A SMALL DESK IN A CORNER
OF A ROOM CAN INSTANTLY
ADD INTEREST AND A SENSE
OF PURPOSE.

WALL SCONCES

THE GORGEOUS TRADITIONAL FRENCH WALL SCONCE is the perfect option when you need or want to light up a small room, a narrow hallway, or add some mood lighting. Many years ago we began picking up antique wall sconces at *brocante* shops and antique markets; and now have them dotted all over the château, although not all of them have been wired in. I have wall sconces in many of my bathrooms flanking the mirror above the vanity and I have popped battery-operated globes into those that either have not been able to be wired in or are still waiting to be done. Fortunately fabulous remote-controlled, battery-operated 'candles' can now be bought online. ➤ The size of the wall sconce makes it perfect for smaller spaces. It can be used as the primary source of light or to accompany other lights already in place. These wall lights come in various materials for you to choose from. ➤ At Bosgouet we have collected dozens of beautiful little silk ruched shades for the sconces as the old ones more often than not come without the shades. These are one of those things that you always see at antique markets and *brocante* shops and are usually very reasonably priced. Look out for them on your next trip to France or make a special visit to the famous markets at Clignancourt to scour through the acres of stalls. ✿

WALL SCONCES PLACED
IN THE RIGHT SPOT CAN ADD
GENTLE AMBIENT LIGHT TO
ANY ROOM.

BERGÈRE CHAIRS

IS THERE ANYTHING QUITE AS VERSATILE AS a *bergère* chair? With its exquisite enclosed, upholstered body, upholstered back and armrests on an upholstered frame, often with an over-upholstered seat, this French armchair is a statement piece in any room. ⤛⤜ The chair may be moulded or carved and made of wood such as oak, beech, walnut or mahogany, very often with an immaculately waxed finish. This charming *chaise* may also be painted or gilded, and sometimes even has little padded elbow rests atop the armrests. ⤛⤜ The *bergère* is mostly fitted with a loose, but tailored, seat cushion as it is primarily designed for lounging in comfort. Historically this 18th-century piece was a *meuble courant*. It was intended to be moved around the room, or house, to suit the convenience and decor changes of the owner rather than being permanently positioned in one spot. Recently, we took all manner of *bergère* outside under the linden trees and set up mini seating areas for a large wedding at Bosgouet. ⤛⤜ Re-covering *bergère* chairs has become a favourite hobby of mine. After I pick up a tatty *bergère* from a *brocante* or Les Puces (they're a great size for popping in the back of the car with ease), I revel in finding a fabric for this new member of the family. I've covered my *bergère* chairs in very formal silks, in checks, in Designers Guild fabric (more suited for children) and even in differing fabrics on the back, front and arm rests. ⤛⤜ I can't paint or draw to save myself but boy, oh boy, can I have fun with a chair! I have great aspirations to learn how to upholster – I've even bought all the tools my friend Julie told me I would need to become a student under her tutelage. However, I've found a wonderful upholsterer near Bosgouet and have become somewhat hooked on the thrill of delivering a funny old chair and then returning later to take my new friend home. ✿

BERGÈRE CHAIRS

Opposite
A BEAUTIFUL UPHOLSTERED
CHAIR FLANKING AN
OAK COMMODE IN THIS
MANOR HOUSE. IT MAY BE
IMPRACTICAL FOR THIS
COMMODE YET IT CREATES
A GLORIOUS LITTLE
FURNITURE VIGNETTE.

Above
FINDING A SUBLIME PIECE OF
SILK DAMASK OR FABRIC THAT
SPEAKS TO YOU IS SUCH A
THRILL. THIS SALON FEATURES
AN EXQUISITE SINGLE
PERIOD CHAIR.

TAKE AN OLD CHAIR AND TEAM IT
WITH A FABRIC THAT SPEAKS TO
YOU. PLACE IT WHERE YOU WILL
SEE IT EVERY DAY – A NEW FRIEND
WITHIN YOUR WALLS.

LA
CHAMBRE

LA CHAMBRE

always feel very privileged when friends take me on a tour of their house – especially if they have decorated themselves, and their home is not simply an interior designer's showroom. It says something about the depth of a friendship to be taken right through the house where you can't help but gain inspiration – and more often than not a deeper understanding of the people who live there. ❧ I remember being taken into bedrooms I'd never seen before in a friend's château in Normandy. We had been having a lovely afternoon chatting about our kids and our lives over copious cups of herbal tea. The day was hot but not in the salon of this 16th-century château. The thick walls protected us from the still heat of the late summer. ❧ My friend asked me if I would like to look at some of the bedrooms, particularly one that still had the original 1804 *Retour d'Egypte* wallpaper covering her walls. We made our way up the stone-and-iron staircase. I was thrilled. I had been to this château for beautiful, formal dinners and lunches but had never been upstairs before. It struck me as we entered the bedroom how simple it was and how perfect was its wallpapered canvas. A beautiful oak French bed that some lucky guest had recently slept in was tossed with crumpled linen but we were there to see the magnificent original wall coverings – nothing more and nothing less. ❧ I asked my host if she minded me taking a few shots, telling her how I loved the truth and beauty of the moment and setting. I'd entered a room of real living. There was nothing prepared or made up. It struck me as a poignant moment of realisation that we all have ruffled, slept-in beds and hand towels strewn across splashed vanities, and yet we apologise constantly if an unexpected friend arrives and our homes don't look picture perfect. I never have a magazine-ready home. With four children, a dog and a very messy husband I learnt a long time ago to sit back, take a deep breath and live with the chaos. ❧ However, there's nothing better than that feeling when you stop on the threshold of a doorway, look inside and breathe deeply, and everything feels right in the world. ❧ I love to pull a bedroom apart, clean it from top to bottom, make the bed with crisp white linen and arrange freshly picked flowers in vases on the bedside tables. When we have guests I fill the ensuite with embroidered damask towels topped with beautiful lavender soap and shampoo, preferably homemade. My armoires always contain white cotton robes, a small ironing board, an iron, distilled lavender ironing water, a soft white waffle cotton linen bag, a clothes brush and a good variety of hangers. ⤳ Traditionally the French boudoir was adjacent to the bedchamber of a lady of nobility and formed part of a very private grouping of rooms where she bathed and dressed. Later the boudoir became a private drawing or sitting room and was used for other activities such as needlework, reading, or perhaps spending time with a lover. ⤳ When we first arrived at Bosgouet a historian from the village came to have lunch with us. As we walked over every inch of the château, he explained that the boudoir was not only a space within a large country house where a woman's private sitting room or salon was situated. Apparently, the word 'boudoir' came from the French term *bouder*, to sulk, and was originally a room for noble ladies to withdraw to and indulge in a good sulk! ⤳ With that in mind I went about creating my ideal boudoir at the château, a place where I could escape to and indulge in the fine art of the sulk! I used layers of fabrics and different materials and added an Empire sideboard fitted with late 20th-century French porcelain sinks that sit snugly into a white marble top, with oodles of storage room underneath. French windows look out onto the manicured garden and it really doesn't matter if it is raining, sunny, snowing or blowing a gale. This room brings me great joy every time I use it and as I bathe I am reminded how lucky I am to be the custodian of this grand old house. ❁

Overleaf
NICK AND IREIDE'S
INCREDIBLE BEDROOM COVERED
IN WALLPAPER.

LA CHAMBRE

Left

I LOVE THE LOOK OF
A HAPPILY SLEPT IN MESSY
BED AFTER A GOOD
NIGHT'S SLUMBER.

Opposite

EVEN MODERN FRENCH
BEDROOMS ARE MULTI-
LAYERED, WITH BEDHEADS,
CUSHIONS AND THROWS.

LA CHAMBRE.

ARMOIRE

THE ORIGIN OF THE FRENCH ARMOIRE DATES back to before the 16th century in France. The word loosely describes any type of wooden cabinet with shelves, and also refers to a cupboard or wardrobe. Armoires were originally used by skilled artisans who stored the tools of their craft in them. These exquisite and often elaborate handcrafted cupboards were an individual art form and an armoire often bears the signature or mark of the artisan in the design carved into the wood. Historically the armoire is said to be a descendant of the chest of drawers. ✍ There are many styles of armoires – from intricately carved and inlaid wood wedding armoires of centuries ago to the practical mirrored door armoires that I find particularly useful in the guest rooms at Bosgouet. They give an authentic feel to the already beautiful rooms, with their parquetry flooring and French windows. I also have a huge marriage armoire on the main bedroom corridor that houses all my starched white linen, pillowcases and hand towels. It has shelves and a few secret drawers where I keep a supply of beautiful soaps. ✍ The armoire is the perfect piece for those living in a small, city apartment who want to inject a French show-off piece into the main living area. It's equally as practical and beautiful in period homes that lack space and storage. It will add an interest and anchor to any room and is just as happy and at home in a bedroom, bathroom, hallway or kitchen. Think out of the box with the armoire. It can hold a multitude of goods and serve a multitude of purposes, and brings great joy in any French-inspired space. It really does not matter where you put an armoire – it will sink its heavy old feet into your floors and be right at home immediately. ❀

EVERY CHAMBER AT CHÂTEAU
BOSGOUET HAS AN ARMOIRE.

Opposite

I LOVE TO STYLE AN ARMOIRE
WITH BEAUTIFUL PIECES
COLLECTED ACROSS FRANCE.

Below

MY FRIEND JANE FOUND THIS
BEAUTIFUL NORMAN ARMOIRE
SOON AFTER SHE MOVED
TO FRANCE.

LA SALLE
DE BAIN

LA SALLE DE BAIN

There is something so beautiful about the old porcelain sinks of yesteryear. The first time I entered a perfect Parisian apartment near *Le Jardin de Luxembourg* I was instantly smitten with the beauty of the bathrooms. Old white porcelain stand-alone vanities with beautifully crafted modern tapware had the design of a bygone era. There were superb French oak parquetry floors in a herringbone pattern, white Italian tiles in the shower and French windows with original joinery. Stunning! ✽ French inspiration in the bathroom can be as simple as a collection of beautifully displayed French products. Think *Durance*, *L'Occitane*, and handmade soaps from a French farmers' market. Add beautifully laundered and stacked towels, and an antique silver dressing-table set, polished to perfection and used as a display rather than for its original practical purpose. ✽ When decorating a French-inspired bathroom, aim to combine boldness with serenity and comfort. You can be a bit quirky and try things that don't affect the rest of the house, such as buying a piece of furniture that you really love, adding a basin and making it the vanity. Or think about using an open cupboard with a beautiful French fabric ruched below the basin or a very formal marble-topped Empire piece with white porcelain sinks. If you have the space, an armoire gives instant French appeal. I love the look of a chicken wire front with gathered or ruched fabric behind the wire to conceal the inner contents. For the ultimate French provincial look you could install uncoated brass taps, which will develop a lovely aged patina as time marches on. Or a classic twin lever tap with white porcelain knobs and a bridge is always beautiful. ✽ If you are redoing a guest bathroom and have the space, put in a luxurious claw-footed bath with a gorgeous chandelier above it and a huge gilded mirror on the wall. You could add a superbly upholstered chair next to the bath and place a stack of towels on it. Dress the window with billowing curtains and fill the bathroom with beautiful objects such as cut lead crystal bowls with silver lids. This won't do as a practical family bathroom but it would make a gorgeous addition to a French-inspired home and could become a personal space for long luxurious baths. ❧

TO EVOKE FRENCH STYLE IN
A BATHROOM, CLASSIC SIMPLE
LINES WORK BEST.

Opposite

A SMALL STOOL OR CHAIR
IN THE BATHROOM CAN HELP
TO GIVE PERSONALITY TO AN
OTHERWISE UTILITARIAN SPACE.

Overleaf

WE HAVE USED EMPIRE
SIDEBOARDS TO CREATE
BEAUTIFUL CLASSICAL VANITIES
IN THE BATHROOMS SINKING
PORCELAIN SINKS INTO THE
MARBLE TOPS.

SIGNATURE FRENCH SCENT

WHILE THE ORIGINS OF FRAGRANCES STRETCH back as far as the most ancient civilisations, it was in dear old France that the personal use of scent was transformed into the industry we know today. In fact, the use of personal scent began with the French court. The French royal house was looked on as a centre of culture, and whatever was deemed fashionable at court gradually spread to the wider society. ➤➤ Scent has the great power to transport us to another world or time. It can lift our mood. It can evoke cherished childhood memories; or can simply add the finishing touch to an outfit, or indeed a home. While there are hundreds of different fragrances emerging each year, there are only a few that truly stand the test of time. ➤➤ The historic fragrance houses of Paris produce many of the most enduring scents and while I love a Cire Trudon candle and a Durance room spray, nothing really compares to my own personal scent, which makes my friends and family exclaim, 'Ohhh, I'm in Jane's home!' ➤➤ My personal scent is a *mélange* of lavender oil, beeswax, turpentine and linseed oil. It signifies layers of love as I clean, polish and arrange. Once I arrive in France, I'll fling open every window and let the sweet French air dance over every space in my home. It doesn't take long for the scent of Bosgouet to find her balance. ❀

USE CIRE TRUDON FOR A
SIGNATURE FRENCH FRAGRANCE
FOR YOUR HOME – SUBLIME.

Opposite

CIRE TRUDON IS BEST
KNOW FOR ITS FRAGRANT
CANDLES BUT THEIR
COLOURED TAPER CANDLES
CAN ADD A DEFINITIVE TOUCH
TO A TABLE, SIDEBOARD OR
WALL SCONCE.

SIGNATURE FRENCH SCENT

195

LA CUISINE

LA CUISINE

The French have a very distinct style when it comes to the kitchen. *La cuisine* has practicality and usefulness but also a beauty all of her own. Over the years I've gained inspiration from grand château kitchens of friends to the tiniest *la cuisine* in Parisian apartments. They are always functional and practical but ooze with French flair and flavour. It might be hand-painted cupboards in a muted duck egg blue, or a row of perfectly polished copper pots lined up or hanging upside down like a military manoeuvre awaiting instructions. ➤ Often the first thing that hits me when I enter a French kitchen is the workhorse – the stove – where all the magic happens. I don't even have to be in a French home for this inspiration. I have whiled away many happy hours in Paris at the kitchen showrooms and stove stores. *La cornue* with her black cast iron and brass knobs is an absolute favourite of mine. ➤ A kitchen should be a place where the welcome is always warm and real, cooking is pure joy and everyone loves to gather. It might be an old cliché but it stands true that 'the kitchen is the heart of the home'. It is where children sit at the bench over breakfast before school or have afternoon tea at the table with beloved grandparents. It is where memorable family dinners that celebrate and commiserate, dinner parties with friends or simply the nightly meal are prepared and enjoyed. ➤ A French country kitchen is so often charmingly cluttered, with cooking equipment in plain sight and easliy reached. It is both practical and beautiful at the same time. To achieve this look, hang pots and pans on hooks and keep them highly polished. Make use of large jars and other *brocante* finds such as pottery jugs to hold wooden spoons and wire whisks. ➤ The humble rooster is a popular French country motif and no country home is complete without one. Look for a beautiful French fabric of a rooster print in blues and greens, with a splash of yellow and red. Search local antique markets and *brocante* shops for copper baking pans in the shape of the bird or perhaps a painted serving platter. I found a glorious cast-iron rooster when we first moved to Bosgouet and he lives in pride of place on the windowsill of one of the six sets of French windows that are in my basement kitchen. ➤ Vintage canisters, particularly in bright red, cream and white make a lovely display. Add layers of French-imported or

Previous leaf
TODD AND AMY'S KITCHEN NEAR
HARCOURT IS A COSY PLACE
TO CHAT.

French-inspired linens, such as tea towels, tablecloths and aprons. There is nothing quite like the colours of provincial linens. The unique textiles of Provence with their rich colours, striped patterns and olive prints make a wonderful statement. ⟩ I love the way you can mix and match as many Provençal patterns as you like within the same family of colours, whether you choose a bright blue and yellow colour scheme or a more subdued set of hues. This palette of Provence is inspired by the surrounding countryside and includes the inspiration of nature – sunflower yellow, sea blue, brick red, olive green, stone grey, lavender purple, and soft creams and whites. Colours often appear in pairs, such as red/white, blue/white, yellow/blue and yellow/olive. ⟩ I often mix the palette of Provence with delicate floral fabrics in purples and pinks. A big comfy chair layered with quilts and cushions, a wooden table with a tray for serving tea and a good book complete the scene. All these elements will make your kitchen an inviting space for friends and family to gather and be nurtured. It's simply the nature of the style! ⟩ I have a dream that one day I will create a perfect kitchen in Paris. There will be a place for everything and – much to the absolute pleasure of Pete after years of exasperation – everything will be in its place. There will be drawers based on late 18th-century Parisian joinery, with sealed plastic inserts for every flour, grain and ingredient I will ever need. Smaller spice drawers will sit under heavy white marbled bench tops cleverly designed to look like Victorian cornice. Every modern convenience will be carefully camouflaged so that the beauty of *la cuisine* is never compromised by the harsh reality of modern apparatus. ⟩ A large crystal chandelier will hang low over a long French oak farmhouse table, which will stand on beautifully waxed parquetry floors. The china and crystal will bring me absolute joy. Each object in this kitchen will speak volumes about a lifetime of inspiration from friends and family, who have so selflessly shown me their style, character and Frenchness throughout my mad love affair with France. ⟩ *Ma cuisine* will be a beacon of environmental responsibility. Recycling will be of paramount importance and specially designed bins will adorn the kitchen cupboards for easy recycling of paper, cardboard and glass. Living in Paris will allow me to shop on a daily basis, just as I have been doing in Normandy and Melbourne for the past thirty years. I'm determined to

have a well-organised, -designed and -styled fridge so that every time I open it I will become inspired by the produce that greets me and ideas for evening meals will simply pop into my head. I've visited the kitchens of many Michelin-star chefs over the years and this fridge beauty has been a recurring inspiration from some of the best kitchens in the world. ✤ My kitchen will have a few cannot-do-without elements, including three different-sized cast-iron cooking pots, an espresso machine, coffee bean roaster, coffee bean grinder and my KitchenAid Cook. There will be a few beautifully chosen copper pots for display. Included in my joinery will be a small cheese larder with wire inserts in the doors. The two shelves of the cheese larder will pull out for ease of cleaning. I will have specially designed and ventilated drawers for potatoes, garlic, onions and shallots. ✤ Under the main central marble bench will reside wine refrigeration running the full length of the bench. It will be temperature specific for champagne, burgundy, white wine and red dessert wines. I think I'd like to have these fridges behind moulded doors in keeping with the rest of the kitchen. ✤ The windowsill overlooking the inner courtyard of the traditional Haussmann building will house my essential herbs of fresh mint, parsley and chives. These plants will be watered daily using an exquisite little watering can bought on *Rue du Bac* at *Le Prince Jardinier*, a wonderful collection of gardening paraphernalia. ❀

Overleaf

THESE CHARMING KITCHENS
ARE PACKED WITH TONAL
CROCKERY AND GLASSWARE,
OODLES OF FRESH PRODUCE
STORED IN BASKETS AND
A WOODEN CHEESE CASE.

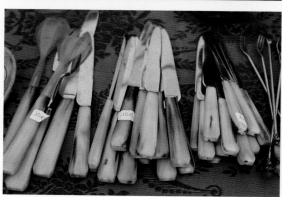

CLASSIC WHITE TILES,
COPPER POTS AND BROCANTE
FINDS IN A FRIEND'S KITCHEN
IN A NEIGHBOURING VILLAGE.
THIS PETIT CHÂTEAU CAME
FULLY FURNISHED AND FILLED
WITH HOUSEHOLD GOODS.

LA LAVERIE

LA LAVERIE

All over France in *brocante* shops, village *foires à tout* and antique shops you will find piles and piles of heavy French-embroidered linens that have been kept immaculately for generations. You may even find napkins or sheets with your own initials carefully embroidered on centuries-old sheets or napkins. ➤ Wash, dry, fold, hang. Repeat and repeat and repeat! Laundry may not be the most enjoyable chore of the day but we can certainly increase the pleasure by creating a beautiful space to work in while we clean clothes and fold linens. ➤ The laundry has often been overlooked when it comes to home decorating. But more and more we are seeing laundries designed with beautiful tiles and luxurious fixtures. One of the nicest and most inspirational ideas I have seen for a French-style laundry was an antique pastry table in the middle of the room, which was used as a folding table. It gave the laundry such a great focus. Having a gorgeous central piece like this to anchor the room makes *la laverie* something special. A large armoire can be used to create a similar effect. It can be fitted out with wicker baskets as a facility for sorting dirty clothes and linen, with the upper shelves storing laundry powders, soaps, fabric softeners and other laundry essentials. A large piece like this has the capacity to house all those things that make their way to the laundry – sewing box, shoe polish, first-aid kit, spare globes. The list is endless. ➤ Think about investing in very good lighting and add some artwork to the wall, even something as simple as a poster translating French washing instructions! Large glass jars with lovely labels in French can be used for powder, pegs, lost socks, pure soap flakes and bars of laundry soap. BHV and other *droguerie* stores have a beautiful range of wooden brushes and cleaning tools that are not only practical but will give your laundry that French style you are looking for. A copper measuring scoop for your laundry powder will give you an instant French note. ➤ An essential in your French-inspired laundry is a stack of freshly laundered and starched linen hand towels. Have them sitting there so that when guests come you can grab a little pile for the powder room. ➤ A ceiling drying rack that comes down by pulley is a useful addition and a lovely way to give a laundry a French feel and sensibility. You could buy a beautiful wooden French ironing board – they look so much nicer than the modern steel ones. Attach a lovely brass hook on the wall of the laundry to hang it on while it's not in use or, if your laundry is large enough, leave it up. ⤙ My suggestion is that next time you put a load of washing on, look around *la laverie* and consider how you can add some style. There are so many things that can be done to improve the space that don't have to cost a fortune. Just a little inspiration and creativity will have you enjoying separating your colours from your whites! ⤙ Most of my French girlfriends are pretty finicky about their washing. They don't like to use harsh chemicals because they cherish their skin, which they take great care to maintain. One friend is a great believer in using natural herbs. Christelle dabs essential oils onto a piece of gauze and tosses it into the machine with the clothes. Perhaps you need to add a dash of peace and calm to your household? Try adding chamomile. Christelle also uses lavender washed and dried with her loads. Tie some up in a piece of gauze and throw it in with the washing. ⤙ French women believe in preserving linens so that they last a lifetime or longer. So they are careful about using stain-removing techniques and always use mild and gentle detergents on their clothing. They hand wash anything delicate to preserve the quality for generations. ⤙ Isabel uses lemon juice and the sun. 'For delicate whites with stains I like to use a mixture of two parts lemon juice and one part water and let the stained item sit in the sun for a few hours. After its sunbaking, hand wash. Lemon is a natural lightener and so is the sun. It is also a natural germ killer.' I keep a huge earthenware bowl of lemons in the laundry as my secret stain fighter. They look gorgeous and smell divine. Plant a lemon tree in your garden to ensure a plentiful supply or use two Versailles-style planter boxes outside your laundry door. ⤙ Isabel went on to say that her *belle mère* had another natural stain-removing technique. She mixes sea salt with a mild powdered detergent in a small, shallow basin of water, places the cloth or item on top of the mixture and sets the basin in the sun. After an hour or so she checks the stain and gives it a gentle scrub. If it needs to sit longer – even up to twenty-four hours – that's not a problem. These mixtures are not harsh and abrasive and will not ruin clothing like bleach or another hard chemical mixture would. ⤙ The best rinse aid or fabric softener you can use is white vinegar. It kills germs and will rid your clothes of any souring (from being left in the machine too long). Vinegar can also help rid your clothes and machine of built-up residue left behind by harsh laundry detergents or fabric softeners. Washing your darks with vinegar added helps preserve the colour longer and keeps the colours from bleeding. Look out for a vintage bottle to store your vinegar in at *brocante* shops, auctions or online sales sites. ➤ If you don't like the smell of vinegar, don't worry – it soon dissipates. However, I have made scented vinegar by adding a few drops of lavender essential oil. The French love lavender and lemon for laundry. And like lemons, lavender is also a disinfectant. ❧

LE JARDIN

LE JARDIN

The French see outdoor spaces as an extension of the living area. It could be a small space with a wrought-iron table and chair propped under a century-old tree or a classic orangerie or conservatory. There are so many effortless ways that you can create a beautiful outdoor room that will feed your French soul. At Bosgouet we have a garden of marked contrasts. The formal terraces and garden rooms give way to the wilder areas within the forests and the relaxed casual areas under the 300-year-old linden trees. ➤ Look for outdoor pieces at *brocante* shops and antique markets. Think urns and iron settings, planter boxes and statues. Fountains are a wonderfully French feature that work exquisitely in an outdoor garden room, whether covered or open. A pergola with creeping vines, roses or wisteria is superb for al fresco dining and creates an anchor where family and friends can eat together under the stars. Another wonderful place for interaction and entertainment is a *pétanque* court. We built a pergola at Bosgouet next to the *pétanque* court and outdoor pizza oven to create a new dining, gathering and cooking space within the *potager* garden. It has beautifully enhanced the relaxed outdoor dining atmosphere we love on those long, warm summer evenings when the sun doesn't say '*bon nuit*' until after 11 p.m! ➤ If you are lucky enough to have a conservatory or greenhouse, then grow lemons and limes in traditional Versailles planter boxes on wheels that can live outside in the summer and inside in the cooler months. You will never again be cursing that you forgot to buy limes for your G&T, not to mention the divine citrus blossom that can be picked to make herb posies to give to friends or popped in your powder room. ➤ One of my favourite places for French inspiration in the garden is at Le Potager du Roi at Versailles. The King's *potager* is an authentic, inspirational experience. You can really see the way things have been done historically – trellising, espalier planting, Versailles planter boxes – as well as the varieties of trees available. Whether you're planning a garden on a grand or small scale the ideas will flow freely after a day there. ➤ For more truly inspirational garden room ideas visit the incredible Château Champ de Bataille in Normandy, created by Parisian interior designer Jacques Garcia. You should set aside a whole day to explore and take photos so you can implement some of Monsieur Garcia's ideas when you get home. ⤳ There are many other gardens that I visit in France for inspiration including Villandry in the Loire and Miromesnil in Normandy. If you want inspiration for a home *potager* or need ideas for garden vignettes that are easy to emulate, these are the places to go. ❦

LE JARDIN

Overleaf

A GARDEN THAT TELLS A MILLION
STORIES NEAR HONFLEUR, WITH
BEAUTIFUL COLOMBAGE NORMAN
HALF-TIMBERED ELEMENTS.

TOPIARY

WHEN WE FIRST ARRIVED AT BOSGOUET WE KNEW that we wanted a garden and that one of the formal elements we would employ would be topiary. Topiary with its formality and structure creates beautiful outdoor rooms for living. ⤜ The topiary at Château Bosgouet is mainly in the form of the geometric structure rather than that of the fanciful. If I'm ever looking for inspiration, I love to visit the garden of famous interior designer Jacques Garcia at Château Champ de Bataille. There is a wonderful topiary walk of lions majestically overlooking hedged pathways there. ⤜ Derived from the Latin word for an ornamental landscape gardener, *topiarius*, topiary is something I never imagined would interest me. However, I've become the *topiarius* at Bosgouet and I've grown to love looking at the trained perennial plants with their clipped foliage and inspecting and plucking the twigs of trees, shrubs and subshrubs to develop and maintain clearly defined shapes. ✿

Overleaf

TOPIARY ADDS STRUCTURE AND
A FRENCH NOTE TO A GARDEN.

FRENCH DOORS AND WINDOWS

IS THERE ANYTHING MORE FRENCH THAN FRENCH doors and windows? The first house Pete and I ever renovated was a weatherboard miner's cottage in a little side street in leafy Armadale, an inner-city suburb of Melbourne. We wanted to bring light into the bedrooms from the side of the house, where there was only a narrow strip of ground a little over a metre in width. One Saturday afternoon we found ourselves at an auction where we bought French doors that were originally part of the Royal Women's Hospital in Melbourne. They were huge, heavy doors constructed of individual, single-paned pieces of etched glass and wood. We decked the side of the house and fitted a set of doors into each room, which created the illusion of more space when the French doors were open. ➤ When we first bought Château Bosgouet I would daydream about opening the windows in every single room each morning. Of course in reality I never opened every window – it would have taken all day. But I do love to start the day by flinging open the windows in my bedroom and bathroom. I put our pillows on the window ledge and leave them to bake in the early morning sun. ➤ French doors date back to the early 17th century and originated as windows that reached to the floor and led onto small balconies. The focus was on symmetry, proportion, regularity and geometry. Windows built into doors allowed people to have light in their homes for a longer part of the day. This was, of course, very advantageous before electricity but continues to be so today. Light can be brought into hallways and interior rooms that otherwise would not have windows. ➤ The doors usually come in pairs with glass panes that extend for most of their length. Over the course of time, they have become widely popular because of their multifunctional uses and beauty. They are a popular choice for many because they bring light into a room and work functionally as a door. Another great advantage is being able to create a breeze through the house after a hot day or to air a home after it has been closed up for a long period of time. The very first thing I always do when I arrive at Bosgouet is to throw open the windows in the main reception rooms to let the sunshine in and get my house smelling like springtime once more. ➤ The oldest original French doors were originally made of wood and wrought iron. Today they are made with many different materials, including wood or rigid PVC, although aluminium is sometimes preferred because of its lightweight quality and strength. We have many friends who have updated their French doors and windows with this aluminium alternative. They still look very nice and have the added benefit of being draft proof and hard to destroy. But nothing gives me quite the same 'I'm back in France' feeling as the original heavy oak doors and windows at Bosgouet, with their beautiful latches and knobs. ✿

I REMEMBER THE FIRST TIME I SAW THE FAÇADE OF THIS GORGEOUS CHÂTEAU IN THE HAMLET OF JONQUAY. I JUST KNEW WE WERE GOING TO HAVE LOVELY TIMES TOGETHER.

NOTHING SAYS FRENCH STYLE
LIKE FRENCH DOORS OR
WINDOWS. IT'S A SPECIAL PART
OF LIFE IN FRANCE.

FRENCH DOORS AND WINDOWS

OFF TO THE MARKET

here's no place on earth like Les Puces de Saint-Ouen at Clignancourt, which arguably has the best shopping in the world. Within the space that makes up Les Puces there are many different markets where you will pay a fraction of the price that you would pay at home from a dealer or interior designer. Each market has a totally different flavour. Some sell high-end antiques and others look like a tip truck has simply up-ended its load onto a stall. ⤳ If you want to shop for real bargains I encourage you to head along Rue des Rosiers to the very end of Rue Paul Bert. I promise that you will not be disappointed. You will find a city of music, tables set up with dealers sharing meals, playing cards or just smoking and chatting. You will find yourself entrenched in the haggling, bargaining and negotiating. ⤳ Les Puces is the real deal. Every weekend, thousands of people wander the little streets and alleys, hunting through stalls piled high with bric-a-brac and admiring the displays. It is a flea market experience like no other where you are sure to find a treasure that you will keep forever. To me, a visit is the perfect way to spend a day. ⤳ What I love best about Les Puces is the side that many people don't get to see. It's not picture perfect in the slightest but it's where dealers from every corner of the globe come to shop and local dealers trade with each other. Friday is dealers' day at Les Puces. If you are a dealer or shopping as a decorator, it's a great place to check out. Make sure you have a business card to get in. ⤳ If you are not a dealer or decorator, you can visit the markets on:

- Saturdays from 9 a.m. to 6 p.m.
- Sundays from 10 a.m. to 6 p.m.
- Mondays from 10 a.m. to 5 p.m.

If you plan to buy at the markets, I suggest contacting a shipper such as Hedley's Humpers beforehand. They can give you tickets to mark your purchases and will pick them up the next day. Carrying a shipper's book has the added bonus of the dealers taking you very seriously. ⤜ One time I took a group of American guests on a full day tour of Les Puces. I picked them up at their Paris hotel and spent the entire day showing them every inch of the market, teaching them how to haggle and not to appear too excited. They bought quite a few items and sent them back to the States. One of them has since contacted me to tell me she had returned three times since our visit and has not only furnished her entire home but the homes of two of her friends! Our day together had led her down the road of interior decorating and now she has a whole new career. ⤜ Another grand-scale antique market is held *en plain air* at the Deauville racecourse. It really is a wonderful market to attend and over the years I have picked up so many incredible pieces. I once bought sixty place settings from the original *Le Train Bleu* restaurant. The restaurant had been renovated and there at the market were all the original silver pieces – cloches, trays, cutlery and sauciers. It was an Aladdin's cave; and perfect for the wedding I was hosting at Bosgouet that summer. ⤜ When visiting any market, don't be afraid to get right in among it all, dig under tables, move things in boxes, and be sure to ask the dealer for a discount. They expect you to haggle. You'll find the atmosphere intoxicating!

Clignancourt Flea Markets
Rue des Rosiers, Saint Ouen 93400 Paris
marcheauxpuces-saintouen.com

Hedley's Humpers
6 Boulevard de la Liberation, 93284 Saint-Denis Paris
hedleyshumpers.com

The French Table
Château Bosgouet, Village de Bosgouet, 27310 France
thefrenchtable.com.au

My French House Chic tours include visiting *brocantes*, shopping for fabrics and seeing gardens. It's everything you need to make your home perfectly 'French house chic'.

SOURCE BOOK

ANTIQUES

FRANCE

Folle du Logis

Le Village Saint-Paul, 25 Rue Saint-Paul, 75004 Paris
levillagesaintpaul.com/la-folle-du-logis-en

Go to Folle du Logis and enjoy rifling through their antiques and high stacks of French plates, serving pieces, glassware and other curiosities.

Virtuoses de la Réclame

5 Rue Saint-Paul, 74004 Paris
levillagesaintpaul.com/virtuoses-de-la-reclame-en

This is worth a visit if you're looking for antiques, vintage posters, old café pitchers and memorabilia.

AUSTRALIA

FRANQUE

597 Malvern Road, Toorak, Victoria 3142
franque.com.au

This is a beautiful space where hospitality reigns. They have a carefully selected range of antiques, as well as Cire Trudon candles and some of the nicest French accessories in Melbourne.

BOOKS

FRANCE

Librairie Galignani

224 Rue de Rivoli, 75001 Paris
www.galignani.fr

The French-polished wooden shelves here hold an impressive collection of around 50,000 titles. Besides the selection of English titles (divided into fiction, politics and history), there is an incredible fine arts department as well.

Librairie Gourmande

92–96 Rue Montmarte, 75002 Paris
librairiegourmande.fr

This two-storey bookstore has an extensive collection of cookbooks, as well as new, used and rare books. Go to the upper floor and have a look at the hard-to-find oversized books by European chefs. Even if you don't read French, a flick through the thousands of beautifully photographed recipe books will have your tastebuds dancing all the way to the market to pick up produce and try out new ideas.

Shakespeare and Company

37 Rue de la Bûcherie, 75005 Paris
shakespeareandcompany.com

American George Whitman opened his bookstore in 1951. It is still in operation today and is a favourite haunt of mine. Whitman's store was originally called Le Mistral but was renamed Shakespeare and Company in 1964 on the 400th anniversary of William Shakespeare's birth in tribute to Sylvia Beach's original store. Today, it continues to sell new, second-hand and antiquarian books, as well as providing a free public reading library. I love the shop's motto written above the entrance to the reading library: 'Be not inhospitable to strangers lest they be angels in disguise'.

Taschen

2 Rue de Buci, 75006 Paris
taschen.com

Taschen is an arts book publisher with an incredible array of coffee table and design books. The Taschen bookstore in St Germaine has always been a firm favourite in our family. Pete and I are avid book collectors and Taschen always inspires us. One year while visiting Paris I bought so many books my checked baggage was over at the airport. So I gave all the books to my sister while I checked in and then carried them on board as my 'light reading'.

COOKWARE

FRANCE

Atelier des Arts Culinaires

111 Avenue Daumesnil, 75012 Paris

leviaducdesarts.com

This shop specialises in copper cookware made in their atelier, which is located just under the viaduct within Viaduc des Arts, in front of the Gare de Lyon. They also re-tin copper. It was after a particularly rambunctious romp through Les Puces in Paris that I visited Atelier des Culinaires with the oversized copper sauté pan I had purchased from Les Puces. It was in desperate need of re-tinning and a French friend had advised me that the atelier was the only place to take my new sautéing friend.

La Cornue

54 Rue de Bourgogne, 75007 Paris

lacornue.com

La Cornue is a French oven and cooking range manufacturer, founded in 1908 by Albert Dupuy. It currently produces three ranges of oven: Château, CornuFé and CornuChef. Dupuy founded La Cornue in order to create ovens that used a new type of natural gas and produced a much more effective oven than the others available at the time. Long have I dreamt of a La Cornue oven and on several occasions have attended cooking classes so that when I eventually am the proud owner of this incredible machine I will be completely au fait with her capabilities.

E Dehillerin

18–20 Rue Coquillière, 75001 Paris

eshop.e-dehillerin.fr

E Dehillerin is a day out by itself. Brace yourself, step inside and check out two storeys of cramped aisles packed with cookware and specialty gear. The staff is well-informed but don't let them talk you into something expensive just because they recommend it. The store is famous for its gorgeous copper, and the plastic pastry scrapers marked with their logo make inexpensive and excellent gifts for cooks back home. My favourite purchases over the years have been little copper butter dishes and a double copper saucepan with a white porcelain insert for making delicious buttery emulsions such as hollandaise sauce.

MORA

13 Rue Montmartre, 75001 Paris

mora.fr

Pastry chefs come from all over the world to visit MORA, which has a great selection of tart and cake moulds, whisks and spatulas. It also has the best selection of chocolate moulds in Paris. It's my go-to place for tart tins, moulds and madeleine tins. I remember after my first ever trip to Bordeaux I visited MORA to buy the adorable copper moulds to make the exquisite little canelés made of egg yolks and rum.

DESIGN

AUSTRALIA

Greenfield & Hunter

7c Avenue Rd, Frewville, South Australia 5063

greenfieldsa.com.au

Greenfield & Hunter have an extensive range of fabrics, wall and floor coverings, furniture and lighting available through interior decorators, designers, and architects. However, members of the public are welcome to make an appointment to visit their showroom.

Gaudions Furniture Melbourne

1001 High Street, Armadale, Victoria 3143

gaudions.com.au

Gaudion Furniture has been providing quality furniture and accessories to create beautiful living environments since 1992, working directly with clients, select interior designers and architects. Pete and I bought our dining room table from Gaudions. It's a classic parquetry topped table with extensions that happily accommodates twelve. Our table sits quite authentically within the walls of Château Bosgouet and has hosted hundreds of dinner guests over the years.

LUC.

15 Castray Esplanade, Hobart, Tasmania 7000

lucdesignstore.com

LUC. offers a beautiful range of homewares, furniture, art and fashion with a focus on high-end design. It is a wonderful concept store where the owner's motto is, 'Love what you have in your home'. I love this store for that motto alone and I think about it before every purchase.

FRANCE

Flamant

8 Place Furstemberg, 8 Rue de l'Abbaye, 75006 Paris

flamant.com

Flamant is a multinational interior and home decoration brand, with headquarters in Geraardsbergen, Belgium. The company has stores in Belgium, France, Germany and

Italy and operates a wholesale network of about 500 multi-brand stores worldwide. Their fabulous collection consists of furniture, home accessories and decorations. We first saw Flamant at the Maison & Objet biannual trade fair in Paris and were enamoured with their collection, which ranges from dinnerware to dining tables, bed linens and sofas. The brand also has a paint collection. The style is described as a combination of classic and modern, charming and bohemian and has a real French sensibility.

Merci Paris

111 Boulevard Beaumarchais, 75003 Paris

merci-merci.com

Merci is one of the most eclectic general stores in Paris. Located in the heart of the trendy neighbourhood of Le Haut Marais, Merci features a great variety of goods – from interior design to fashion, two cafés and one restaurant. Downstairs you will find a nice selection of wooden cleaning brushes and gadgets for the kitchen and laundry. I love dropping in and picking up a stack of lovely laundry and kitchen brushes as well as linen tea towels to give as gifts.

UNITED KINGDOM

Petersham Nurseries

Church Lane, Petersham Road, Richmond TW10 7AB

petershamnurseries.com

A trip to Petersham is always a good idea. This beautiful garden centre has an amazing range of plants and flowers for sale, plus a tempting range of gardening tools. Some of my favourite products can be found here, including Astier de Villatte white/grey pottery and prettily wrapped soaps, Cire Trudon scented candles and other small goodies. We love to visit just before Christmas to do a spot of festive shopping and have lunch at their idyllic café.

FABRICS & WALLPAPERS

AUSTRALIA

Boyac

30 Cremorne Street, Cremorne, Victoria 3121;

15–19 Boundary Street, Rushcutters Bay, New South Wales 2011

boyac.com.au

Boyac offers a large range of textiles, wallpaper and lighting, with a strong focus on craftsmanship, and their experienced staff are always happy to provide expert information and

advice. I would often pop my head in the door of their Melbourne store to see what inspiration I might find. I loved sorting through the large wicker basket of remnants by the door and finding leftover pieces of fabrics that were perfect for a small upholstery job or a cushion.

Cloth & Paper Studio

9 Lyell Street, Fyshwick, ACT 2609

clothandpaperstudio.com.au

Cloth & Paper Studio is the place to go in Canberra if you're looking for textiles, wallpaper and soft furnishings. On a trip to Canberra to visit the 'Palace of Versailles' Exhibition I found myself, as I often do, searching for a piece of fabric to take home as a souvenir. Cloth & Paper Studio had just the piece for my collection. When I get home I always pin a small note on the fabric so that when I come to use it, I can remember where it came from.

FRANCE

Manuel Canovas

6 Rue de l'Abbaye, 75006 Paris

manuelcanovas.com

All my old favourites are housed here, including fabrics by Colefax and Fowler, Jane Churchill and Manon, to name just a few.

Le Marché St Pierre

2 Rue Charles Nodier, 75018 Paris

marchesaintpierre.com

This legendary fabric store has by no means lost the charm of years gone by. You might be forgiven for thinking you have landed in another time as you walk across the highly polished wooden floors or pay at the antique cash registers where employees sit in mahogany cash register booths. Once you have made a selection and the fabric has been cut, you will be expected to pay, so don't let them rush you. Purchasing a piece of fabric that can be used to make cushions or upholster a precious piece of furniture inspires happy travel memories every time you see it.

Pierre Frey

1 Rue Furstenberg, 75006 Paris

pierrefrey.com

Pierre Frey is a luxury design house, an inspirational, family-owned business with a proud tradition. Founded in 1935, the company designs, creates and manufactures fabrics and wallpapers in the purest French tradition. The company's rich collection (of no fewer than 7000 items) includes not only Pierre Frey designs, but collections from the company's other three prestigious brands: Braquenié, Fadini Borghi and Boussac. I bought a piece of Pierre Frey years ago and took it home, popped it in a cupboard and promptly forgot about it. A decade later I found the glorious egg-yolk damask piece and recovered two lovely little children's wing back chairs.

Rue Hérold

8 Rue Hérold, 75001 Paris

rueherold.com

Located between the historic Palais Royal and the fashion district of Montorgueil, Rue Hérold is a store with a mission. Founded by Charlotte de la Grandiére, a former stylist for fashion and design magazines, the shop offers a carefully coordinated selection of fabrics, sewing notions, ready-made and made-to-measure cushion covers and curtains, bags and zip cases. It is a wonderful place to buy a memento of your Paris visit. And it's easy to pop a cushion cover or a small bag into the bottom of your suitcase to take home.

Tissus Reine

3–5 Place St Pierre, 75018 Paris

tissus-reine.com

If you're looking for toile de Jouy this is the right place. They offer large selections for cushions and bed covers and you'll also find loads of pale jacquard fabrics that make excellent upholstery fabric. Their prices are slightly higher than other shops, but you don't always find the same selection and quality elsewhere, and here you can still find a bargain.

Yves Delorme

45 Rue Croix des Petits Champs, 75001 Paris

yvesdelorme.com

You can find Yves Delorme stores all over the world and online. The company is known for its beautiful bed and bath linen, sleepwear, soaps and house fragrances. The days were short, cold and so gloomy during our first winter at Bosgouet that I decided I needed to brighten up our bedroom and bought beautiful sheets, a valance and doona cover from Yves Delorme. The quality of those red damask-like sheets was so outstanding – they never faded or frayed – that I handed the set over to one of our daughters to use when she moved out of home.

Zuber & Cie

28 Rue Zuber, Rixheim, 69170 France

zuber.fr

The Zuber & Cie factory is a French manufacturer of painted wallpaper and fabrics, and claims to be the last factory in the world to produce woodblock printed wallpapers and furnishing fabrics. Buy a beautiful panel of woodblocked wallpaper to take home and frame – it's a work of art. On my last visit I picked up a piece of exquisite embroidered

silk with beading and elaborate needlecraft techniques. The factory still employs the traditional hand-printing techniques in use since its establishment in 1797.

UNITED KINGDOM

Tissus d'Helene

Unit 421, The Chambers, Chelsea Harbour, London SW10 0XE

tissusdhelene.co.uk

In this tiny little shop, hidden away in Chelsea Harbour you will find a beautiful selection of furnishing fabrics and papers from niche suppliers that can sometimes be hard to come by. Look out for vintage-style papers from Adelphi Paper Hangings, chic use-anywhere prints from John Stefanidis and beautiful old-style silks from Taffetas Dubarry.

HOMEWARES

AUSTRALIA

Christofle

11 Bay St, Double Bay, New South Wales 2028

christofle.com

Christofle is a French manufacturer of fine silver flatware and home accessories. It was founded in 1830 when jeweller Charles Christofle assumed management of a jewellery workshop belonging to his wife's family. Among Christofle's product lines are silver picture frames, crystal vases and glassware, porcelain dinnerware, and silver jewellery and holloware. Pete and I decided to make one major purchase on our honeymoon back in 1990. Something we would use every day and have forever. It was our wedding gift to each other – twelve place settings of Christofle. I now live a dozen or so kilometres from the factory and have included this gem in my French House Chic shopping week tours.

Durance

1022 High St, Armadale, Victoria 3143

durance.com.au

Durance is a family business based in Grignan, Provence, selling skin care, candles and home fragrances. They take their inspiration from nature, especially the plants and flowers of the region. I love Durance room sprays and I leave the pillow sprays on bedside tables for guests to use as they wish.

FRANCE

A. Simon

48 Rue Montmartre, 75002 Paris

The stock is constantly changing in this shop where you will find an especially good selection of glassware and heavy-duty, professional-quality white French porcelain. I bought my French onion soup bowls in various sizes in this lovely store and it is where I first fell in love with the gorgeous French brand Pillivuyt. Their exquisite quality porcelain has been gracing French tables since 1818. I love that their pieces transfer directly from oven to the table.

Astier de Villatte

173 Rue Saint Honoré, 75001 Paris
astierdevillatte.com

Astier de Villatte is renowned for its signature approach to ceramics. Handmade in the workshop that was once occupied by Napoleon's silversmith, each piece is one of a kind. The company also makes a beautiful range of candles that are housed in either hand-blown glass or ceramic. I have always been drawn to this exquisite store piled high with ceramics inspired by the 18th and 19th centuries.

Au Petit Bonheur La Chance

13 Rue Saint-Paul, 75004 Paris
aupetitbonheurlachance.fr

Filled with old French charm, this shop has lots of linens, café au lait bowls and kitchen knick-knacks. If you can't make a leisurely visit to a flea market or *brocante* on a Saturday morning but would love to take home a treasure, then this is the place to go. My first purchase at this store was a pair of beautifully embroidered white linen pillowcases that still grace our pillows.

Le BHV Marais

52 Rue de Rivoli, 75189 Paris
bhv.fr

The BHV Marais offers various departments across its eight floors and in its smaller, specialised shops nearby. It also has three other stores, each of which, like the main store, comprises several departments. It is a great place to go for cookware and homewares, hardware, books and fashion. They have a wonderful hardware section in the basement, but I think my favourite area is the droguerie. I love the beautifully crafted wooden brushes, dusters and cleaning implements of all kinds. I dream of the day I will visit BHV to purchase everything I need for my Parisian apartment!

Buly 1803

6 Rue Bonaparte, 75006 Paris
Website Buly1803.com

This small apothecary is a favourite place to shop in our family. The girls and I love to pick up brilliantly packaged scent, soaps and custom-blended potpourri. Presents from here won't fail to delight. The staff are all trained in calligraphy and will address gift labels by hand.

Cire Trudon

78 Rue de Seine, 75006 Paris; 11 Rue Sainte Croix de la Bretonnerie, 75004 Paris; 24 Rue de Sèvres, 75007 Paris
trudon.com

Founded in 1643, on the threshold of the reign of Louis XIV, Cire Trudon is the oldest candlemaker in the world still active today. Four of the five senses come to life every time I enter Cire Trudon. Choosing a candle for my powder room is such a treat and never disappoints. Take your time to look, feel, smell and hear the gentle sonnet of the candle as it burns and flickers, and imagine it filling your home with the scent of centuries past. I always have a scented Cire Trudon *Prolétaire* (Lily of the Valley) flickering away in the powder room at Bosgouet and am delighted that I can now buy them at Franque in Melbourne.

Faïencerie de Gien

78 Place de la Victoire, 45500 Gien, France
gien.com

The Faïencerie de Gien is an earthenware factory in Gien, France founded in 1821 by Thomas Edme Hulm. If you love pretty china, then you can't go past Gien where you'll find a good selection of beautiful pieces. You can also visit the museum, which is situated next to the shop. My personal favourite in their range are the divine blue and white signature plates. It is a gorgeous gift to buy a friend with their initials inscribed on the plate.

La Verrierie

15 Rue du Louvre, 75001 Paris
laverrieredesign.com

Push open the gate and visit this dark shop hidden in a courtyard. You're expected to head towards the back and comb the aisles for yourself where you'll find glassware and earthenware. Take bubble wrap with you so you can safely tuck an exquisite piece of cut lead crystal into the corner of your suitcase.

UNITED KINGDOM

AG Hendy & Co

36 High Street, Hastings, East Sussex TN34 3ER

aghendy.com

We found this shop when driving through rural England. It has been lovingly restored and now sells new and vintage brushes, enamelware and china for the kitchen. This store also runs the most interesting workshops. It's almost like a little finishing school for adults! Tablescaping is one of the many workshops on offer and, with years of experience as a stylist, Alastair Hendy gives the attendees a modern twist on how to entertain in the 21st century.

PASSEMENTERIE

AUSTRALIA

Decor Design Centre

299 Fitzgerald Street, West Perth, Western Australia 6005

decordesign.com.au

I first heard about Decor Design Centre on a family holiday to Margaret River in Western Australia. I was looking for a beautiful tassel to complement a piece we had recently bought and a lady I met while doing yoga overlooking the Indian Ocean at Bunker Bay suggested this was the place to go. They have a lovely collection of *passementerie* and I was not disappointed.

FRANCE

Declercq Passementiers

15 Rue Etienne Marcel, 75001 Paris

declercqpassementiers.fr

You can buy some of the best *passementerie* in Paris at Declercq Passementiers. You can also buy a wonderful kit to make your own tassel key ring – a truly inspirational gift for anyone who loves French style. On the first Thursday of every month, Declercq artisans offer demonstrations on workbenches and looms in the store; however, you do need to call and reserve a place.

Les Perlés d'Antan

142 Rue des Rosiers, 93400 Paris

marcheauxpuces-saintouen.com

Located in the Clignancourt flea market just beyond the city's boundary, this is the place to buy beautiful vintage *passementerie* – brocades, buttons and ribbons. I love looking for antique tassels that I can tie on an old key that sits happily in a chest of drawers or armoire. Look for large tassels in colour combinations you love that will add a splash of colour to any room.

UNITED KINGDOM

VV Rouleaux

102 Marylebone Lane, London W1U 2QD

vvrouleaux.com

Go to VV Rouleaux to buy some of the best *passementerie* in London. They sell over 5000 luxury ribbons, tassels, braids, flowers, feathers, cords and other trimmings in hundreds of colours. They also offer a free colour guide to help you navigate their products.

UNITED STATES

Hyman Hendler & Sons

142 West 38th Street, New York 10018

hymanhendler.com

This is a great source for *passementerie* in New York. Established in 1900, the store is renowned for its ribbons and trims. If you love pretty things, then you can never go past bringing home a tiny tassel or piece of braid to use on a project at a later date. I often look at a lamp that has a fringing of tassels and think of the time I bought that particular trim in New York. It makes for a much more interesting souvenir.

Schoen Trimming & Cord Company

151 West 25th Street, New York 10001

cordsandtassels.com

This store has been in business for over seventy years and is also worth a visit if you're looking for *passementerie* in New York. While Schoen is known mainly for its academic tassels and cords, it's a wonderful source for other trimmings and tassels as well.

AUCTION HOUSES

AUSTRALIA

Abbeys Auctions
482A Station Street, Box Hill South, Victoria 3128
abbeysauctions.com.au

Abbeys Auctions deals in whole house lots, deceased estates, unpaid storage, antiques, jewellery and collectables.

Christopher Bragg Auctions
194 Christmas Street, Alphington, Victoria 3078
cbraggauctions.com

Christoper Bragg specialises in house lots and I have had always had success here with blue and white pieces and gilt clocks. We managed to be the winning bidders on a lovely gilt clock, with a rural scene of lady lazing atop the clock face.

E. J. Ainger Auction Rooms
433 Bridge Road, Richmond, Victoria 3121
ainger.com.au

It was at this auction house as a child that I made my first purchase. My antique teddy bear collection began here! Ainger's have both weekly and special sales, with catalogues available online.

Leonard Joel
333 Malvern Road, South Yarra Victoria 3141;
39 Queen Street, Woollahra, New South Wales 2025
leonardjoel.com.au

Leonard Joel deals in art, antiques, jewellery, collectibles and interior furniture. My earliest memories of visiting an auction room with Mum and Dad are at Joel's original auction house in St Kilda.

FRANCE

Hôtel Drouot
9 Rue Drouot, 75009 Paris
drouot.com

Hôtel Drouot is an enormous auction house in Paris. It consists of sixteen halls, which host over seventy independent auction firms. Every week Drouot publishes the only magazine dedicated to public auction house sales of collectable art and objects. This weekly publication gives the latest news on the art market, announcements and presentations of sales to come. It is available every Friday at kiosks all over Paris and through subscription. If I'm in Paris on a Friday, I'll pick up the catalogue and find myself a brasserie, order a coffee and pour over whatever is on offer. You can subscribe to the Drouot catalogue and place absentee bids online.

UNITED KINGDOM

Chiswick Auctions
1 Colville Road, London W3 8BL
chiswickauctions.co.uk

Chiswick Auctions deals in antiques, as well as modern items and designer goods. It's always such a thrill when a parcel arrives from an auction house in a far away place.

UNITED STATES

Paddle8
30 Cooper Square, New York 10013
paddle8.com

Paddle8 is an online auction house founded in 2011, which deals in paintings and sculptures, furniture, antiques and decorative objects, jewellery and memorabilia.

Doyle Auctions
175 East 87th Street, New York 10128
doyle.com

Doyle Auctions deal in fine art, jewellery, furniture, decorations, Asian works of art, coins, stamps and rare books.

NEW ZEALAND

Dunbar Sloane

7 Maginnity Street, Wellington 6011; 375 Parnell Road,
Parnell, Auckland 1052

dunbarsloane.co.nz

Dunbar Sloane deals in art, antiques, decorative art, artefacts,
toys and dolls, wine, militaria and colonial collectables.

Mossgreen-Webb's

23–25 Falcon Street, Parnell, Auckland 1052

mossgreen-webbs.co.nz

Mossgreen-Webb's deals in fine art and single-owner
collections. I first came across Mossgreen when I was doing

a series of book talks in New Zealand. It's a wonderfully
eclectic auction house to scour through.

Smiths Auctions

88 Montreal Street, Sydenham, Christchurch 8023

smithsauctions.co.nz

Smiths Auctions deal in surplus stock, and estate and
household furniture. The weekly auction on a Friday is -
for the most part - very utilitarian, however, if you scour
through the household section you may just find a hidden
treasure. Many people don't like this type of auction but this
is where the true finds can be had, as often a little pearl has
been overlooked in the bottom of a box.

ONLINE SHOPPING

1st Dibs

www.1stdibs.com

Rather than your typical online store, 1st Dibs is more
a marketplace where a world of antique stores, consignment
stores and other purveyors of fine things list their wares. Sign
up to their newsletter or check back often lest you miss out
on that one-off piece of perfection.

Bluefly

bluefly.com

Bluefly offers a little bit of everything from couches to
cashmere, selling previous season's stock at heavily reduced
prices. If you love it, buy it because once it's gone, it's gone.
It's a great site to sign up to and they will send you alerts.

D. Porthault

dporthault.com

At the turn of the 20th century, Daniel Porthault opened
a small lingerie boutique in Paris. In 1920, his wife Madeleine
convinced him to expand. At a time when France and the
world were sleeping on traditional white and ivory linen,
Madeleine and Daniel introduced a new style of bedding –
printed sheets. Since then the company has produced
countless beautiful collections of bed and bath linen,
sleepwear and napery.

ACKNOWLEDGEMENTS

Without the tireless hand-holding of my incredible publisher, Kirsten Abbott, this book would not be here today. Thank you once again, Kirsten, for putting your blind faith in my ability to produce this book. Thank you also to Tahlia Anderson and Brigid James for your patience and meticulous assistance during the editorial process. One of the most exciting moments in this project was when I first saw Daniel New's design. Thank you, Daniel, for your exquisite talent. To my dear friend and incredibly talented photographer Robyn Lea – what fun we had running all over France shooting these beautiful spaces together.

Thank you to the following friends for allowing us
into your private spaces:

John and Linda Barrett

Nick and Ireide Walker

Laurence and Thierry Achard de la Vente

John and Doris Wolfe

Jane and Stephen Hiscock

Julie Currie

Thank you also to the following hotels and private
apartments in Paris and Normandy:

Hôtel Relais Christine

L'Hotel

Ferme St Simeon

Haven, Paris

First published in Australia in 2017
by Thames & Hudson Australia Pty Ltd
11 Central Boulevard Portside Business Park
Port Melbourne Victoria 3207
ABN: 72 004 751 964

www.thameshudson.com.au

ISBN: 9780500500965

National Library of Australia Cataloguing-in-Publication entry
French House Chic/Jane Webster
9780500500965 (hardback)
Australians–France.
Interior decoration–France.
Decoration and ornament–France–Influence.
France–social life and customs.
Webster, Jane, author.

Cover: Pattern from the 'Documents XI' collection by Zuber & Cie.
Design: Daniel New / OetomoNew
Editing: Writers Reign
Printed and bound in China by Imago.